Beyond Roses
An Obligation to Speak

Finding Voice for Conversations

Judi Moore Latta

Beyond Roses—An Obligation to Speak

Copyright © 2020 by Judi Moore Latta

ISBN: 9781705562505
Imprint: Independently published
Silver Spring, Maryland

Library of Congress Control Number: 2019918201

Printed in the United States of America
First Printing. 2019

Editor: Raven Padgett
Cover design: Bilalmalik101

Dedication

For those who have been silent too long.

For all who have taught me to speak and to listen … especially those who have done it with patience and love.

For Dorothy and Larry who first showed me the rose and For Joe who reminds me it lives.

A few words about this book...

"*Beyond Roses—An Obligation to Speak* is a collection of beautifully written personal memories and insightful observations addressing one of the most challenging issues of our time. Judi Moore Latta's accounts of her own encounters with racism as a child and as an adult are poignant and often heart-wrenching. Yet she has an unbridled sense of optimism and a deep conviction that mutually respectful, honest discourse focused on bridging social divides is a primary way in which this blight on our society can eventually be erased. This book can serve as an inspiration and a guide for all who share that view. A visionary, Dr. Moore Latta sees our collective efforts as a beautiful rose taking root against a towering brick wall – an emblem of what is possible, if only we will try."

Catherine R. Gira, Ph.D.
(1932 – 2019)
Former President, Frostberg State University
Former Chair, Maryland Humanities Council

"… We must all join in the deliberate effort to decorate our time in history with music, stories, images and voices that reflect who we are, who we are becoming and have the potential to become. Judi Moore Latta's masterfully detailed storytelling style helps us learn how to tell our own stories and make our conversations rich and meaningful."

Lebo M.
Producer, Arranger
The Lion King

Contents

*"I will bring you a whole person.
You will bring me a whole person,
And we will have us twice as much,
Of love and everything."*

– Mari Evans

Part I:

On Petals, Stems and Thorns

"We must speak with moral authority because silence is not an option…"

–Rev. Dr. William Barber

"We needed a record … of our experiences, lest the day come when our children found our story implausible."

–*The Coming*
Daniel Black

Introduction

T HE ROSES, MORE than anything else, made me think about
writing this book: the rose in Mom's yard, the rose in Dad's
desert, the rose guarded in each person's heart that renders her
silent and reluctant to answer the door. These roses—complete with
hardy stems and thorns, fragile petals and blooms—made me do it.

I couldn't be quiet and watch while so many people were dying,
hurting, crying, forgetting, fading, missing, being demonized,
separated, disconnecting, falling, dropping, losing, trying desperately
to be human ... and some of us could remember or could see. In the
face of resurgent racism and growing contempt, with the evidence of
emerging hatred and repeated bigotry, it is clear that some perspectives have been completely devalued and too many people have felt the
grip of animosity. The stories are staggering. People of color are being
killed for no legal infractions, pulled over and stopped because they
"look suspicious," locked up or locked out of the country because of
who they are. Sanctioned from the highest levels of government, the
familiar narratives associated with racial difference have marginalized
individuals, have labeled them animals, and have traumatized whole
communities. These narratives are dangerous. As long as I can be a
witness to uncover truths hidden in plain sight and help the healing, I
need to speak and tell the stories I know. I cannot be silent.

All of us have fears and prejudices, and all of us have been guilty of having a narrow perspective. I must have the courage to pull off the petals and go beyond roses to tell the stories others may not tell but someone needs to hear. Finding one's voice and being brave enough to use it, not just in opposition, but in conversation with someone who is different from oneself is imperative in the 21st century. I must, in my Mom's words, "Do what the Spirit says do."

Much of what we learn about being in the world, we learn by the end of our childhood. By then we know how we perceive and treat people, how we think and talk about them and ourselves, how we handle relationships and use them to survive. We don't absorb much beyond that, but we later learn to hide what we know, to bury what we believe and to ignore what we see. We become callous and indifferent.

Matters of race and identity separate, silence and render our challenges invisible. In fact, when we talk about race across racial lines, we don't tend to tell the truth. Issues that are difficult to solve without reallocations speak in different ways to groups that have been either socially neglected or privileged. They describe in different ways the places that are considered taboo and the citizens that are considered pariahs. They reverberate in different ways the attitudes that are entrenched for as long as people are old. Still, there is value in speaking and in having conversations. It makes us human together.

Narratives can heal, histories can teach and accounts can restore, but unless there is at least one willing spirit to tell stories and one to listen to them no one can have hope. And without hope, positive change cannot exist. The loosely connected reflective stories in this book are my truth. Yet, they are both personal and collective. They capture moments I remember, as well as ones I claim about "racial rules." A story in this collection may describe my experience with stockings but it is as much about lessons of privilege someone else learned from Band-Aids or crayons or ointment or makeup. A story in this collection may mention my seeing police tape across a piece of artwork, but it is as much about the struggle of another person of color. It is the tale of being unfairly criminalized or made a victim in a system that insists upon silence.

Countless times someone has told some version of these stories in a hushed whisper or in a secluded place. I believe it's time for them to be in the open. They are designed—like the stems of roses—to prick the conscience, touch the soul and create a set of "a-ha" moments that make it hard to walk past hope without taking notice. This is not a book simply about racial slurs and white hoods. It is about what well meaning people ignore and allow to happen because they don't want to be uncomfortable. The idea is to read, feel and be encouraged to search for your own truth to continue the conversation.

This is a guide to take action and make that happen.

"I had to stand awhile in the darkness, and then gradually God has given me light. But not to linger in. For as soon as that light has felt familiar, then the call has always come to step out ahead again into new darkness."

–Mary McLeod Bethune

Rose Poem

To be a rose should be enough…

Little flower, fragile and fragrant,
Lovely and beautiful,
Wanting to bloom while someone tries to grip you tight and
squeeze.

You disappear and return
        Ever so often in the fullness of time,
        Even in darkness when moments stand still,
        In full proclamation to what is beyond.

You come as a witness
        To what is silent,
        Screaming to be told,
        In search of a conversation.

You bring
        Blood with your thorns,
        Sinew with your stems,
        Bones with your roots.

In breath and spirit
You have but to smile and look at the sun
And
You
Will
Blossom!!

The Rose

MY MOTHER ALWAYS had plastic flowers in our front yard. Yellow roses and red carnations were her favorites that adorned the flower box nestled beneath the kitchen window. Year round they "blossomed" thanks to the frequent sales at Walmart and the coupon specials promising two bunches for the price of one.

The neighbors had real ones, but Mom's plastic flowers never faded with the change of seasons and never dropped petals in the worst of storms. This was good, she explained, since it meant she could save both time and money—very important to her—when it came to beautifying her yard.

Always blooming, the flowers perked up at attention. The neighbors all knew the secret and kept it like they were protecting gems in a bank vault. Nobody commented on Mom's artificial flowers although they watched closely for those rare occasions she would switch them out and go for something purple or lime green, two of her favorite colors.

Mom chose plastic because real plants wouldn't grow for her. She had tried azaleas and other bushes native to Tallahassee yards and even crocuses that florists claimed needed very little attention. "They grow like weeds," people said, but not for Mom. Her plantings fell like lead—literally. People in Oak Knoll knew LaVerne Moore had a lot of gifts, but a green thumb was not among them.

So, it is a curious thing that five years after her death the first rose appeared. A <u>real</u> one. It bloomed right outside the window beside the room that held her favorite chair, not far from the box beneath the kitchen window. If the rose that grew had had a tongue, it would have licked mockingly at the place where the plastic flowers had always stood and where now an empty space lay dormant.

A single red blossom appeared in June—around June 21st to be precise— Mom's birthday. What made it stand out was that it was not on a bush. Budding and near perfect with petals tightly folded around a voluptuous center, the red rose grew alone.

Appearing to come out of nowhere, it meandered as if defying its location and insisting that it be noticed. It made its way up the brick wall of the house, straining to reach inside. The single rose, soft and delicate, too precious to resist yet too filled with thorns to hold, grew in the yard alone.

Who knew how it got there, what chance planting may have happened a decade before, why it took so long to emerge? Who could think about what hands had nurtured and prepared it for when it would spring up, Topsy-like, untamed and loose? Clearly alone in the yard, it carried with it the stubbornness of resilience that had been my mother's hallmark. It strained its neck up and leaned its back down so that it bent—much like Mom's osteoporosis had rendered her frame into a curve. In a strange way, it carried her name.

Things had changed around this house from the time when a family lived in full celebration of life. Now the house was empty. Grass grew a little higher, dust gathered a little longer, windows opened a little slower—as only an occasional visitor came to air out the mildew and throw out the DampRid. But the rose growing by the window was a reminder that no matter how things changed, how few people came in and out, how infrequently somebody appeared, the spirit of a living force prevailed. A history that could not be smothered emerged from this place. Stories of tiny victories and whispered secrets that scratched away ugly precedents had to be told. Tales from childhood of cultural triumph and quiet humanity staring down racial hate had to be repeated. There were stories of proud men and women with hope who refused to accept a status quo. There were also stories of young people who lent their bodies and minds to visible and invisible revolutions and people who offered lessons for new generations. The rose made sure that somebody would remember.

My family visits regularly a few times each year. We've added a new driveway, replaced the old roof, even built a sunroom with windows all around. We've trimmed the great oak tree limbs that menacingly hung over the house and every now and then recalled the hospitality the place once held. These are superficial. More importantly, we've tried to do what the house always urged—to answer our call, to make a place for all people in our hearts, to never just settle, to give until it hurts and to speak to the world and the wind that swirls around us, all things we learned in the place.

Every year since the first rose appeared, an additional rose has come. Last year there were five. Most are clustered together, but each year one grows alone. I can't say Mama is in that one rose, returning to be near, to watch. Neither would I claim that some unexplained reincarnation happens, allowing her to rise up. Yet it wouldn't be hard to imagine that she is there—not with any plastic artificial presence but with a real eye on things—lovely and caring and smiling, reminding us to bloom and spread the word.

Movie Theatre Truth

"In the chill climate in which we live, we must go against the prevailing wind…"

—Thurgood Marshall

STANDING FACE TO face, people can still be far apart. The moment when one becomes personally aware of the distances within privilege can be daunting or can give one a sharp edge.

It was 1954 and the ink of *Brown v Board of Education* had barely dried. In fact, the collective surprise of a nation that would be called upon to change had just begun its more than fifty-year snake-like journey. The old ways were still entrenched. "Separate but equal" not only prevailed as a myth some really believed but "stuck in the craw" of others who knew better. Tallahassee, like the rest of the South, served a bitter pill. At the railroad station, two water fountains—one higher than the other, better maintained and marked "whites only"—reminded people of the order of things. The reminders were everywhere, nothing subtle about the message—separate days at the North Florida fair; separate benches in waiting rooms; separate seats on buses; separate eating places; separate health care; separate public bathrooms; separate schools; separate churches; separate cemeteries. Even the graveyard attempted to devalue Black life by insisting that a dead body deserved restrictions. Absurd jockeying pushed innocence toward experience.

When I was 6 years old, I had not yet realized the cocoon my parents had spun as they tried to protect me from these harsh realities. As faculty members at the all-Black Florida A&M University, they had bought property outside the city limits—a half acre carved out of the Florida forest. They were building a house where an old plantation once stood, in a subdivision that had been advertised in the paper as a "good place for Negroes." Construction of the brick structure that was to be our house was moving well under the supervision of Mr. Chenault, the white contractor in charge. One day, he brought with him to the building site his granddaughters, both my age, and we hit it off immediately, roller skating and hopscotching our way through the afternoon. Hide-and-seek around the big oaks shading the yard made us laugh and talk until we were exhausted. Until that moment.

"We go to the Florida Theatre to the movies," one of the girls said, her eyes dancing with carefree mischief. It was a simple enough declaration, something not unusual for me since going to the movies had been what I had done all my life. In fact, I immediately remembered being dazzled by munchkins from *The Wizard of Oz* and excited by fast moving cowboys and cowgirls who seemed to ride off the screen into the auditorium every Friday night. It was a ritual I knew well. Friday night movies. But it never occurred to me that the movies I had seen had always been in Lee Hall on the Black campus of Florida A&M.

We must have passed by the Florida Theatre a thousand times, as we drove down Monroe Street through the heart of downtown from our soon-to-be new house to the campus. There always seemed to be continuous lines wrapped around the Florida Theatre when we passed, people waiting to get in to see something exciting. So, on the day that my new friend made her declaration I took it in stride.

"We go to the Florida Theatre to the movies," she said from her privileged perspective. And without missing a beat, knowing I had never been inside the Florida Theatre, but not wanting to be outdone nor outclassed, I responded. "I go to the Florida Theatre too."

The laughter was instantaneous, coming from two 6-year-old bodies that had been drenched with centuries of propaganda and insidious treachery. They laughed so hard they could barely contain themselves. In fact, they almost cried. Two innocent girls repeated the words they had heard someone else say, the hurt they had watched someone else deliver, the voice they had witnessed someone else speak. Without a thought, they said, "But the Florida Theatre is for white people."

I was stunned. I had never given it a second thought. It had never occurred to me that the only people standing in those lines circling the Florida Theatre that we drove past every day were white, that the dozens of children waiting to get in were white, that the faces of those eager to see the movies were white. I was shocked by the revelation, but only for a second. From somewhere deep inside, I gave my retort.

"Well," I said. "I went to the Florida Theatre BEFORE it was for white people."

Their faces dropped, their voices silenced, their spirits quieted. Clearly, they had no history or information from which to respond, just as I had none from which to declare another thing. We were all in the dark, but at least for the moment I had won.

First Job

I REMEMBER MY FIRST paying job like it was yesterday, perhaps because it taught me the truth. I was about to enter my senior year in high school in 1965 and no one could tell me I didn't stand on the threshold of "the new age" my Dad told us was coming. My neighbor, Mr. Wallace Burgess, a true maverick of a man, arranged for a summer opportunity at the Florida State Capitol. I would be among a few who would be examined for positions. This was no small thing since at that time only a handful of Blacks had ever worked in the building in an assortment of roles.

A gaggle of lucky high school honor students heard that we would be hired for the summer in paying jobs. Since I was one of those who had been hand-picked, going to the Capitol would give me a chance to get real work experience. I was excited. Preparing for the day was like going to a prom—hair neatly brushed into my signature pony tail, nails cleaned by digging into a special bar of soap I kept under the sink for such purposes and breath freshened by Colgate. Nothing, I thought, could keep me from getting a good placement on this day.

We arrived at the building and lined up against a wall under a cavernous ceiling. Portraits and pomp, as well as scenes of the Everglades, surrounded us like they belonged in the place. More than twenty white kids were there. I was the only Black. We stood nervously as an examiner came down the line, notebook and pen in hand, brow furled, asking the same question and instantly making assignments.

"How many words per minute can you type?"

His question was magic to my ears. If *this* was going to be the way they assigned us to offices and sites within the state government, I was going to be in good shape. After all, I had learned to type when I was 12. In fact, my folks had sent me to a typing class on the campus of Florida A&M before I even reached the seventh grade, because, they said, they wanted me "to have skills." It hadn't been a waste. I had typed school assignments for years, using my Dad's old World War II typewriter, at a time when my classmates were hand writing all their work. I had even been so lucky as to get my own electric Smith-Carona for my birthday when I turned 15 so that I could type poems and letters.

As the examiner made his way down the row, he asked each student, "How many words per minute can you type?" The boy two persons in front me shakily said, "25?" answering the question with a question as though he didn't believe what he said. The examiner nodded and assigned him to the office of the Secretary of State. The next girl's answer to the question was a firm "35." "That's good," came the reply. "You'll work well as a receptionist in the Speaker's office."

Then came my turn. I pulled myself together, prepared to wow the examiner with my answer of "75 words per minute," which I knew was just a modest estimate of what I really could do. I had tested—at least a few times—at better than 80 words per minute in Mrs. Kyler's typing class. I was ready. My answer was certainly bound to land me in the office of the Governor. But before I could say a thing and even before he even asked me the question, the examiner looked directly at me—or perhaps *by* me—and said, "Mailroom." He then moved to the next person.

I was crushed. I had not been asked a thing! I had been assigned to work, without assessment, in a place that required no particular skills and I had more than a few. The examiner delivering the message wanted me to know that he believed me to be less important than the others in the room. He wanted to be sure I did not think myself as good as anyone else. Thank God I knew better. Racism was trying to rob me of the end of my childhood and force me to drop hope, but I had come from a community that believed in fortifying.

It is necessary to understand that at this point in my life, I knew no white people intimately and certainly none by name. Where I went to school and to church and to play I had no contact with any. My education, my recreation, my health and well-being, my very existence had taken place totally in a segregated community where there only were Black people, many of whom had tried to keep us focused on the highest performance standards. While they never spoke of it directly, I now realize they were trying to get us ready for the time we would learn that even when our own high standards mattered to us, they may not matter to others. When I experienced this, my first real contact with white people, and was overlooked for an opportunity to demonstrate my abilities, I learned another hard lesson. I was being introduced to the notion that white privilege allowed mediocrity to take precedence over excellence in a world where claims to the contrary were prevalent.

I went to work in the mailroom, sorted letters for two weeks and spoke to no one—not because I didn't want to but because all the employees there were white men who ignored me, looking *by* me in the same way the examiner had. Even the ones who may have wanted to speak, didn't, perhaps in fear of retaliation from others. At lunchtime each day, I sat alone at my workspace, ate the sandwich I brought from home and read my dog-eared novel.

Since they all knew my routine, it was no surprise when someone tried to disrupt it. Ten days into my sorting job, it happened. As I broke for lunch and opened my book to begin to read, a greasy half sheet of paper stuffed between the pages caught my attention. Someone else had put it there. I didn't know at the time that the words may have come from someone's fear masked as bravado or from another's warped hold on an escaping order. Scrawled in dull pencil was an ugly message. "Nigger, beware the Hunter's Club."

Stunned. Two wrecking balls and a bulldozer seemed to hit at once. I could feel the eyes in the mailroom waiting for my reaction. Every inch of my body wanted to either cry or scream but I refused to give them the satisfaction of my fear. Hollow and shaking inside, I gave no outward clue to how I felt. After a few excruciating seconds, I turned the page, coolly pretending to read my book for what seemed like an eternity. Time stood still. Then when I could, I gathered my things and my dignity and walked out.

White people had never been the barometer of my existence—the determiners of how I saw the world. What they thought had never been central to what I thought of myself. But the words on the note, nevertheless, had stung as they lingered beyond a few moments. While I was not completely deflated, I felt like a balloon out of which some of the air had been sucked. Still there remained my community, my place of refuge where I could retreat, renew and bear witness. It gave me an infusion of oxygen.

I told Mr. Burgess, the same neighbor who had positioned me for the job, what had happened. In careful specifics, the events unfolded and tumbled out in all of their sordid details. I'm not clear what this Black man who had his fingers in many pots across racial lines ever did about the incident and I'm not sure who (including my parents) he ever told, but in the tradition of what my Dad used to call "protection by the village," Mr. Burgess somehow arranged it so that I did not have to return to the mailroom and could spend the rest of my summer in another building.

What is important is the story as I saw it unfold. The tendency, one might think, would be to withdraw—to keep this story, this humiliation, this wound to myself or to tell only those who would recognize it because they had similar stories. But I was changed that day. No illusions. No debilitating anger. No assumptions that this would be fixed right away. In fact, I couldn't really see how this all would end. What remained, however, was what someone once called a "righteous determination" and a resolve to confront my feelings honestly, to speak my truth faithfully and to let my voice be heard whenever I could in the difficult conversations ahead. It would be hard, but it would be necessary to be brave enough to start.

Look Alike

"... We are well adjusted to injustice and well-adapted to indifference ..."

–Cornel West

IN MY EARLY years, I could never figure out why white people said that African Americans all "look alike." After all, we were every color of cream, caramel, chocolate, vanilla, mocha and beyond and were sizes and heights that matched the color range. In my family alone we ran the gamut. My grandmother Cornelia from Cincinnati had the pale hue of a white woman, standing proudly in her stubborn resistance. All the more reason she borrowed a social term from the early twentieth century as she claimed to be a "race woman." As a result, she refused to let any stranger walk between her and her clearly African-featured, honey-colored daughters as the three of them walked down the street. Her husband Sam, my mother's father, boasted about being dark. He never called himself black although he was close to a royal blue. His skin shone like charcoal every time sweat poured from his face and he took a puff from the perpetual cigar hanging from the corner of his mouth.

Other families could claim the same range of visible difference in their lineages. Sometimes these differences were so obvious that folks wondered if different same-surnamed children were really kin. It was not an anomaly because the brutal historical reality of slavery had made it so. Being "African American" meant genes clashed in our veins, doing a poor job of hiding the history of rape and pillory that had violated our ancestors' bodies and defined our looks. In many corners, we had struggled to keep that pillaging from overtaking our minds as much as it had overtaken our bodies. We were African, European, Native American, East Indian, West Indian and Asian in ways that defied description or categorization in a single mold. We were different from each other yet, at the same time, similar to every other human being on the planet. Even though we all shared an ancestry, we were so distinct.

So with all of that, I never could understand why some white folks still said that those defined as Black "all looked alike." How could they confuse a 6 foot 200- pound Black woman having a Nordic nose with one who stood 5 feet 2 inches, weighing barely 100 pounds with features that screamed out her Nigerian Igbo lineage? How could they confuse a light brown, square-jawed, muscled Black youth of 20 with another who had dark skin, a round face and a paunch?

And then one day, five decades ago, I had a conversation with a white girl who was my college roommate for a semester in Virginia. She had come to what was then Hampton Institute from the Midwest in a student exchange program naively in hopes of having a "Black experience" at a college that would be "safe enough." She had been assigned to room with me. Maybe administrators thought I would be a good choice because I had grown up in the segregated South and needed exposure. Or perhaps they thought that as a chapel assistant, my Christian background would make me more tolerant and less likely to attack her during the turbulent times of the 60s. Or maybe they just knew conversations needed to happen and I would speak my mind on issues that mattered. Too often we avoid speaking what we believe in an effort not to offend but I've always tended to hit issues straight on.

She and I got along fine, not chatting too much but enough. We talked about those things that were necessary and realized that we both were English majors and only children, both preferred writing to cooking and both loved poetry and watching dancers who could fly. We heard music differently, however, she on the upbeat, me on the down.

One day as we discussed some of those things, I'm not sure why I said it but I did. "All white people look alike to me." My statement hung heavy on the air as though waiting for an answer that would never come or for an answer that shouldn't. She seemed hurt and genuinely

all people you don't know look alike

surprised by my abrupt admission and for a second I regretted my honesty.

But then a door opened. "Actually," she responded, "Black people are the ones who look alike." Now I was dumbfounded. She must be crazy! How could she even imagine that all the Black folks I knew so well and so distinctively had any resemblance to each other? Couldn't she see that our skin was every color of the spectrum and, therefore, we clearly looked different?

So I said it. "We are not alike at all. Our skin runs the full range." Without missing a beat, she responded, "But your hair is all so similar in color." There it was. I had never thought about it that way: hair color as a way to determine identity. In her youthful exuberance, she suggested that most Black people she knew had dark brown or black hair and that whites she knew were strawberry blonds, dirty blonds, redheads, dusty brunettes or had hair that was chestnut, auburn or ash.

As she talked on and on, I realized I had never even noticed her hair color. If I closed my eyes, I couldn't have told you if she was blond or brunette. In one historic swoop, I realized the problem. I had never paid any attention to the color of a white person's hair and she had never paid attention to the distinctions of a Black person's skin. We had seen past each other through our own lenses, with our own prejudices, from our own histories. We were talking apples and oranges and had missed the discussion about fruit. Yet, like other things rendered invisible by what we assume and what we know, this matter had trickled over into our relationships and had made us blind. It meant we shut down what we learned about each other and what we taught about ourselves. I may have been too young and too immature at the time to realize the limitations of my narrow perspective. Our conversations never went much further. We talked about the superficial and ignored the intrinsic. We missed an opportunity to go beyond the surface to see the heart.

People talk past each other every day, hoping that what they say will be enough to give them some semblance of sanity but never realizing that the talk does not honor the identity or the compassion of another.

Some fifty years later, it surfaced again—the hair color argument that is. In a 2016 lawsuit in Washington, D.C., a young Black woman claimed racial discrimination, positing that she and other Black employees had been fired from their jobs as bartenders because of who they were. The employer, they charged, favored people who were white. The defense in the case, on the other hand, went straight for the hair—arguing diversity and that the owners had made a point of hiring workers who "did not look alike." "Indeed," the defense attorney said, the employer had not been biased because "after all," he had not only hired "blond women" but had hired "brown-haired women" too. He thought the argument was sound enough to use. Of course, he lost the case.

Imagine a world where heart and soul define individuals rather than hair and skin. We have much further to go than where we are … to find out who and what we really look like, to appreciate our humanity, to connect with our responsibility to be. The conversation must continue.

A Hair Story

Y UNCLE DUD had street cred. Even though he had not been elected to run his neighborhood, in the early 1970s he wielded power. He knew how to leverage underworld associations to make them count as real plusses. He knew every kingpin, every gambler and pickpocket, every self-proclaimed revolutionary who inhabited Western Avenue and Central Square in Cambridge, Massachusetts. He knew the law-abiding shopkeepers and the church elders, the working folks and the drifters. And every one of them knew him. They called him "the man."

It would not seem strange for Dudley Moore, a second-generation West Indian, to hold court in the middle of the day in front of a Jewish delicatessen with half of his crew of middle-aged men hanging on his every word and the other half knocked out in a stupor. He was known for conversations. People of all stripes liked him and followed his lead even as he dragged his feet and his dreams behind him. They listened to what he said, perhaps because he had a good heart.

Dudley was my father's younger brother who drank, so different from Dad who had played sports and worked his way through college in the 1930s. Four years younger than my father, Dudley somehow had positioned himself as a defender of reputations—especially his brother's. He had always been proud of his big brother "Os" (short for Oscar) and had never allowed people to bad-mouth him. If they did, there were consequences, everyone knew. Dudley didn't play.

My first full-time teaching job came at the school where forty years before Dad and later Uncle Dud had been students. In 1972, I joined the faculty of Cambridge High and Latin and became only the second professional Black person working at the school. The other was a secretary. Each time Uncle Dud saw me pass his corner perch in Central Square, he boasted to his boys, "That's my girl." In his mind, I was as much his child as my father's.

Guided by the Civil Rights Movement and a flair for the dramatic, I immersed myself in "consciousness," as I regularly referenced the Black revolutionary voices of Malcolm X and Frantz Fanon and combed my hair into a rebellious Afro. My hair, in fact, had become my most obvious personal declaration of James Brown's anthem, "Say it loud, I'm Black and I'm proud." Carefully shaped and mindfully rounded, it spoke louder than I ever could. I claimed and affirmed every strand.

My first time in a high school classroom as a teacher and I was determined to give more than English grammar and American literature. The 9th grade curriculum mandated that the students read, *The Red Badge of Courage* by Stephen Crane. As I led them through the maturation, heroism and cowardice of the protagonist in the book—a white man making personal choices during the Civil War of the nineteenth century, I wanted them to be aware of contemporaneous voices. I assigned slave narratives so they could also know the anguish and triumph of other heroes—Black men and women of the same era. Students loved the juxtaposition. Parents were skeptical. The Irish/Italian principal was less than enthusiastic. Cambridge High and Latin had never been revolutionary.

Then one day, the principal came to my classroom when I was alone planning my bulletin board. He warned me to stay in my place, to follow the curriculum, to leave off teaching about perspectives that were not authorized. I was not surprised and, in fact, was partially prepared with a push back argument of balance. I was absolutely shocked, though, at what happened next. In the midst of the tirade, while he criticized my choices, this middle-aged white man reached across the line marking the boundaries of our individual personal spaces and into my hair.

He touched my hair and let his hand linger too long to be a mistake. He seemed fascinated. Who knows what he thought he was doing? Perhaps his curiosity bested him and pushed him to wonder if my hair offered a clue to me. Was it soft like cotton or rough like wool? Or perhaps he believed the urban legend circulating about Angela Davis— that he might find a gun smuggled into the school in the vast bush atop my head. Or maybe he embraced the racial myth, that he would have good luck by "rubbing a nigger's head." Who knows what motivated him? Whatever the reason, he did it.

And when he did it, the ancestors shivered, my mind raced and I recoiled. I felt violated, but I did not object because I was a new faculty member and my future hung in the balance of a response. After school, I headed home, passing by Central Square. When I saw Uncle Dud in his usual place, something inside me felt obligated to speak. I told him about the principal and the incident.

The next day out the window of my classroom, I saw Uncle Dud on the sidewalk entering my building. He walked like a man on a mission. A half hour later, the principal made his way to my classroom, urgently called me into the hall and apologized profusely.

I never knew what happened when Uncle Dud met the principal, what was said or not, what conversation they had. But something occurred. That administrator changed. He may never have thought it necessary to see another's perspective, to consider how his personal prejudices or fears affected others. But for sure, after the conversation, he thought twice before doing again what he had done.

Nude Stockings

I WENT SHOPPING ONE day and felt the weight of white privilege in T.J. Maxx (the bargain outlet store). The trip was no different from many I had taken before, when I spent minutes searching for a bargain among the handbags stacked carefully in their vegan/non-vegan elegance. Some faux leather choices were the usual $19.99 and other bags stashed among them stood out like elephant's ivory hidden among the plastic. Those were the ones that someone would inevitably snatch up and be willing to pay $99 to get a bargain that would ordinarily have been $300.

The trip was fairly routine. I had not intended to buy anything and was, rather, simply looking to pass leisurely the one hour I had on this Saturday afternoon. And then I came across something I really did need. I hadn't worn stockings for some time. Maybe it was because this was summer 2015—a particularly hot time for the Washington, D.C., metro area. Or maybe I avoided them because I heard a girlfriend eschew stockings, saying she stopped using them when she "learned that Michelle Obama didn't wear them." Whatever the case, I hadn't worn stockings for months.

But now I was about to go to a wedding and figured I needed a pair, if for no other reason than my new shoes would fit better if I had some on. So, what better place to get stockings than a store known for discounts? At least here I could buy ones that would rival the supermarket prices but would have the department store's class. High-end stockings—satiny, ultra-shiny, no-run pantyhose with control top and sheer toe at a reasonable price. I looked on the back of the package to make sure the size was right. A/B would never do since clearly my hips and my fluctuating weight said I needed the next size up.

I searched and found them—a pair of stockings in my size. At the same time, it hit me. With all of the choice and freedom I had to be here in the first place, with all the economic buying power I had from a good job to be able to purchase several pairs, with all the flexibility in time I had to shop leisurely for what I wanted, I was bound by the reality.

The color did it. The choices of the stockings in the bin privileged someone other than me. Nude. Flesh tone. Natural. Probably not intended to give an advantage to anyone, the colors had been chosen and stamped on the packages as though they knew the order of things. They were etched with the history of a country that said that the default position was for someone who looked different from me. That their way was the norm and everything else was an anomaly. The color names on most of the stockings naturally assumed that the buyers would be white. My "nude, flesh tone, natural" skin shouted creamy brown like chocolate chips or Hershey's Kisses. Their "nude, flesh tone, natural" weighed in much lighter.

Of course, there were a few other shades I could buy that really did match my skin: Tan Bronze, Cinnamon, Barely There. But these didn't carry the names that pronounced normality; they didn't use the language that proclaimed a natural place in the order of things. Rather. these other names suggested being on the outside. I thank God I had parents, grandparents and a village who set me clearly in place and made sure I felt good about the image I saw in the mirror, even on my legs. They instilled confidence to help me understand my self-worth. Others haven't had the same grounding.

No one would claim that those who created the colors of most stockings were racist. They probably were good people with good intentions who never gave a second thought to the names. But that's just it. When the physical look that is defined as "normal" is associated with only one race, those outside the definition feel excluded while those inside the definition may be oblivious to the privilege of being considered "normal." The "default" position becomes the "normal" place and consciously or unconsciously that position is granted only to those who are white. The language we use to construct and shape normality becomes central to the way millions of people see themselves and others. That language works its way into our everyday experiences and choices and products and ways of talking about the world. It suggests who belongs and who is on the outside.

Nude. Flesh tone. Natural. The words may be innocent in isolation and may only be used scattered in conversation, but when compounded and connected with skin color bound by race, they become part of an institutionalized system. They reinforce an unequal institutional power. Naming colors on packages of stockings may appear to be a small matter, but it is a matter that reminds us of how much remains for us to do to level the field, scatter the privilege and value all perspectives.

The Obligation to Speak

"A heavy and cruel hand has been laid upon us. As a people, we feel ourselves to be not only deeply injured, but grossly misunderstood ... The great mass of American citizens estimates us as being a characterless and purposeless people; and hence we hold up our heads, ... against the withering influence of a nation's scorn and contempt."

–Frederick Douglass

"I saw a Black man shot down and I cried. Not the first time it had happened, but for me a time when it reverberated."

–Jeffery Weatherford

November 19, 2015

I TALKED TO A brother today who had at least two tongues. He had mastered both so that he had become fluent—bilingual in a way. We sat backstage in Cramton Auditorium at Howard University before a DJ contest and carried on a conversation about his story. He showed me a photo of his artwork, bold and brazen, starkly laying bare a community's raw spots and tugging at wounds that some would rather hide.

He had been beaten. He never knew why. Like so many Black men before him and so many others since, he had found himself at the end of a policeman's billy club and then a Taser. For no reason he knew, he had to stretch for his life, hoping to continue to breathe when somebody misidentified him, "misrecognized" him, "misclaimed" him as guilty of something he did not do. Nobody on the force really explained. And when he demanded to know what drove the two Prince George's County police officers to twist his arms behind his back and wrench them into a hold clamped by iron, they told him nothing. When he insisted that they show their badge numbers, they simply said, "Just call us Sheriff 1 and Sheriff 2."

It happened two years before and like the warning from his middle-class mother about being deferential and respectful when confronted by police, this incident never left him. It hovered there like the stories of Timothy Thomas being shot dead in Cincinnati; Danroy Henry killed in a car pulled to the roadside; Oscar Grant hunted in an Oakland train station; Rodney King beaten by LAPD; Amadou Diallo shot while attempting to pull out his wallet; Abner Louima sodomized by NYPD with a toilet plunger; Sean Bell killed the night before his wedding; Tamir Rice shot by Cleveland cops in front of a recreation center; or the string of others shot in the leg or chest or back. He thought particularly about Prince Carmen Jones, who years before fell victim to a police officer from that same Prince George's County. This young man talking backstage at Cramton described feeling like he had no power when his hands were behind his back. He said he thought he might be on the way to being counted among the dead.

The police never gave him an answer of why he was beaten. Never charged him with a crime. Just eventually let him go. And when they did, they let loose the two tongues. On this day in Cramton I heard them both. One would criticize and fault with the ease of a scholar studying to earn an MFA in art. It was a voice able to speak the historical and cultural legacy of an unnecessary abomination that reverberated in too many Black lives. It was a voice that used a rational argument to move those who talked with him in casual conversation to a new place, as he explained carefully how the criminalization of Black men is systemic. It was a traditional academic voice. And the second voice—the one that emerged later that evening—spoke "hip hop." Defined by the rapping, pulsating, staccato of a man who spit his hurt, pumped his fist and spewed his anger, that voice spoke rage. It too persuaded, but it spoke from a personal place.

Code switching. That's what some might have called what the young man could do. He spoke with two tongues that needed to reach anyone and everyone who felt oppressed, needed a voice or wanted change. One tongue would be for people who negotiated the world with politeness and restraint, who talked from the vantage point of years of fears pushed from the outside in. The other would be for a generation of men and women on the edge—those who heard him from their own vulnerabilities, tired of Black bodies made victims of mistakes, unwarranted aggression and malice.

One voice spoke in private to me backstage before the program. The other spoke in public to the audience of college students who had come for the DJ competition just a few minutes later. Both voices spoke with power saying, "Black lives matter too" in ways huge and clear.

On this night, as the young man prepared to serve as a judge for the DJ competition and talent show, he ate hors d'oeuvres and finger food in the greenroom. What the audience out front did not know was that the young contest judge had yet another voice. He made art. His work was not intended for walls and museums, but for action and real lives. As an artist, he drew what he saw and he knew what he drew. It had the potential to persuade.

The photograph he handed me had a blunt familiarity. The piece he had created had something in common with work by Gordon Parks. In fact, "American Gothic," is the way he identified the work in his photo. It showed his adaptation of Parks' classic of the same name. This mixed media piece made of wood, fabric and old police tape reached seven feet tall he said. He had drawn the full-frontal likeness of a young Black man without facial features, hands raised. Actual yellow tape crisscrossed the work. Surrendering and objecting at the same time, as though ready to bolt and determined to stand at once, as though refusing to settle for something routine, the thin Black man in the artwork stood and the tape constrained.

"It's my thesis," the artist said. "My way of saying something." Loud and insistent, clear and precise, the work showed a Black man caught between the here and now of tragic moments and the historic arc that keeps happening. The photo of the thesis created a visual voice, reminding me that we have averted our eyes too long.

Ringing in my head was the image of Calvin Bess' father in 1967 who had displayed on his lawn a burned-out car that had held his murdered son. Also in my head was the mother of Emmett Till in 1955 as she insisted on an open casket with the body of her mutilated son. "Let the world see what I've seen," Mamie Till Mobley had said. This artwork implied the same haunting refrain: "Let the world see what I've seen." It proclaimed we must say something about what we know.

It's hard to say how voices will speak when confronting a horror, what language they choose to use to describe it, how that language can push someone else to do something or what difference any of it makes. But, clearly, the prism of what language we use has a role in reframing ideas and moving things. One who is born to influence others, to help people shift power relationships, to force them to see in new ways, to use the language they know, must do just that.

We have an obligation to speak, to have more than polite conversations and to use whatever tongues we have available to do it.

Part II:

Story-Hope

As I watched the video of the pint-sized teens with my heart in my throat and my eyes glued on the routine, I had pride, fear and hope as the team members performed, earning their way to another national cheerleading championship.

A Poem: For Jazmine –
A Winner

Little Black girl tumbling on top of the heap…

Let your limbs fly like the wind and your mind speed like a bird.

Let your dreams be bigger than your grandmothers' and heartier than your mom's.

Let your body contort and fling for real purposes beyond yourself.

Let your spirit guide you at every moment as you face the unfathomable.

Let your speech tell the story.

Take care of that voice moving in the night.

Allow it to cry when it is touched,

Bellow when it is wronged,

Soothe when it sees pain,

Speak when there is something to say,

Laugh when you have a chance to leap at the sky.

May you pull with authority,

Listen with compassion,

Maneuver with ease,

Lead with eyes wide open,

Look at the sun and be humbled.

Even when no one hears and everyone passes,

When the wind promises that things will be different and they aren't,

When matters that are ugly take priority,

When all that you see is without hope,

Be the change.

Dance above the small.
Whirl beyond the petty.
Rise over the tightrope.
Find your flip and do it.

The world is waiting.

The Rhoda (Rose) Spirit

"We need a spiritual and moral awakening ..."

–Dr. Cornell West

SOME PEOPLE STANDING guard over themselves and their lives find it hard to hope and to believe God answers prayers and opens doors that lock out truth. They say it's a bit disconcerting to learn that prayer really works and that answers are waiting. Faith and expectation have proven to work as partners of possibility in various religious traditions. Widespread testimonies from those traditions give faith credit for resolving difficult situations.

In the Christian Bible, the story of Peter and the praying people of ancient Jerusalem is one demonstration of the power of hope. The New Testament account tells of people in the house of Mary who are praying for the release of Peter from prison. Of all those present, Rhoda, a servant girl, is the one whose response moves closest toward true hope. Like her name, which means "rose," Rhoda had layers of precious petals (or faith) waiting to be cultivated and turned into sweet possibilities.

Rhoda knew that Peter, a leader of the church, had been in Herod's prison where many had died and from which none had ever escaped. With one more night to live, Peter was in an impossible place— something Rhoda seemed to understand instinctively. As one relegated to a servant's position, she probably knew what it meant to be in a hopeless condition. Who knows, she may have even knelt to join those praying in Mary's home to add her voice to plead with God to be merciful to Peter.

And then came the knock. I can imagine Rhoda went to the door because she was available or because she alone had heard the knock or because she was closest to the door or because, as the servant girl, this was her role. Whatever the reason, she went to the door, and when she heard Peter's voice she was overjoyed. She recognized that voice immediately, perhaps because she had heard him preach or had known him to pray. She may have even sat with him for hours to learn about what he had to teach, paying close attention to what wisdom about God came from his mouth. She knew that voice so she rushed to tell others the good news.

"Peter is knocking. He is here," she said, and, in the process, she forgot to open the door.

"You are beside yourself," they replied, thinking it was impossible. They didn't believe Rhoda that Peter was at the door. But she kept insisting that Peter was the one knocking.

"It must be his angel," they said. She told them that Peter had arrived but people didn't believe her, in the same way they don't believe little Black girls who have no power or privilege; in the same way they don't believe women who have been abused; in the same way they don't believe children suspected of creating tales that make people uncomfortable. Those traditionally considered outside of the power base (in this case, the salvation story) are the least to be believed, trusted, listened to, followed—when, in fact, they have historically been the protectors of the promises.

And the story says, as if she held a rose too precious to touch, Rhoda guarded what she knew, paid attention to what others told her and, for a moment, refused to act on her own faith. She didn't open the door. Yet there stood Peter outside knocking. He had broken enemy chains, escaped certain death and arrived at the house because it was God's will and somebody had prayed it would happen. He had walked out of a maximum-security prison past armed guards but now he could not get through a locked door that belonged to the church.

People stand guard in many ways, hoping to keep out what is uncomfortable or unexpected or different, holding on to the familiar and giving lip service to their faith. They allow others to laugh at and question the experiences they know to be true. They find it hard to hear stories that center people other than themselves. We are they. Sometimes we squeeze so tightly and close our eyes and ears so much that we miss the blessings waiting to enter our lives. We have no clue that what we've prayed to be is actually there.

In the midst of such chaos, on the edge of such doubt, here's wishing for a "Rhoda-spirit" that can not only acknowledge hope, recognize an answered prayer and hear another's story but is willing to open the door when the blessing arrives.

Roses in the Wilderness

"It was St. Augustine who said, 'Hope has two children: anger and courage.' And you have to talk about both of them. 'Anger at the way things are,' the way you grieve deeply, the way you're bothered. ... that looks at things and says this is just not right ... But then you have to have courage after anger to be willing to address it...and the courage to do it with love and non-violence..."

–Rev. Dr. William J. Barber, II

May 2017

THE ATROCITIES ARE so severe and so frequent that it's easy to be dumbfounded. Hard to imagine and even harder to reason how life, so fragile and precious, can be considered so lightly. Sad commentary that only a few people are willing to cross lines to defend the sanctity of people different from themselves. On a Portland, Oregon, commuter train, two girls of color—one Muslim, one not—are verbally accosted by a self-proclaimed white supremacist. Three white strangers come to their defense. Two of those strangers are stabbed to death; the other is critically wounded. A trickle of objections surface here and there across the country but no unified national outrage! Expediency can silence people, especially if the stakes are high. When precious things—like jobs, families, reputations—hang in the balance, then the option to be silent becomes more attractive. When people think their own lives might be in jeopardy if they stand for someone else, they hesitate.

When I think about the men who lost their lives on the commuter train in Portland in 2017, for no reason other than they dared to speak, I think about the resurgence of a terrible reality, a desolate and empty place. It is a place where anger and courage collided. My father heard a story eight decades earlier that points toward how even the most barren of territories can inspire hope and provide fertile ground for roses.

Dad told me that when he was a student at then all-black West Virginia State College in 1932, the world shook. As he sat under the tutelage of a man the students lovingly called, "Prexy," the world around them swirled with hatred. In 1919, Dr. John W. Davis at 31 had become the youngest president in the history of the school and was one of only a few Black men presiding over colleges by the 1930s. As an outspoken advocate of "Negro education," Prexy gave advice, warnings and wisdom and saw himself creating a revolution to combat the surrounding hatred, one student at a time. He knew the world would not welcome his charges and he wanted them to be ready. In the college's mandatory Sunday chapel services, Dr. Davis reminded students that they mattered, that they had God-given power and that they could change the entire segregated South.

It's not clear whether he told them the mantra that so many embraced—that they needed to be "twice as good as a white man to get half as much." If he didn't tell them that, his speeches reassured them that they were "the future." They were studying education, languages, literature, fine arts, natural sciences and mathematics, as well as social sciences and philosophy. One day they would be professionals and they needed to have what Dr. Davis called "social intelligence." They needed to know that they were not alone. He urged them to accept the responsibility to tell the stories not heard in "polite society" and those too raw, too real, too ugly to be told for convenience.

The times were tough. The tensions between races were high. Only a few years out of the post-Civil War Reconstruction era, a string of atrocities and heinous crimes against people who looked like the students stretched from coast to coast. In Alabama, three states to the south of the college, nine young Black men known as the "Scottsboro Boys" had been roguishly arrested and wrongly convicted for allegedly raping two white women—a life or death offense. In Indiana, two states to the west, Thomas Shipp and Abram Smith—two Black men accused of theft—had been publicly lynched. And then in Georgia, a prominent woman college dean—a victim of a tragic car accident—was denied access to the white hospital nearby and, as a result, later died. All of it was tolerated by state and federal officials in their own form of silence.

Prexy at West Virginia State College told these stories, sharing the harsh realities of violent events in daily capsules but reminding students they had both choices and allies. Faced by the reality of traumatizing hell in their lives, their choices were to be silent or to speak. Faced by the same reality, their allies were those who stood with them, despite what might happen for standing.

Silence was not an option and allies were not a gift to be taken for granted. Hard lessons carried bitter truths and demanded that people of good conscience speak on behalf of those who were vulnerable.

On one occasion, Dad heard Dr. Davis tell the story of Bishop Joseph C. Hartzell, a white humanitarian, philanthropist and preacher who lived his conscience and spoke his mind. In the 1920s, Bishop Hartzell travelled throughout Africa—Liberia, South Africa, Congo, Zimbabwe—challenging unfair policies, building undeveloped missions and having a reputation for serving those with little hope. In the United States, he did the same, using every instance he could to speak with courage. According to President Davis, those who knew Bishop Hartzell called him a "friend of the Negro," a label that may have cost him his life.

On the Bishop's 87th birthday, two white men surreptitiously entered his home. Who knows their intent? They may have heard him give one of his unabashedly outspoken sermons about shared fundamental human decency and been outraged or they may have watched as he operated in the Freedmen's Aid Society coming to the defense of Negro youth who had no voice. They may have resented his co-founding Meharry Medical School to educate Negroes or they may have simply broken into his house to steal from him. Whatever the reason, they entered his home spewing hatred and ransacked it; took his watch, $15 and an air pump; and cut his phone lines and then his throat.

President Davis repeated the story many times and, in each telling, he called it "a tragedy of tremendous magnitude." But, at the same time, he called Bishop Hartzell's death "an opportunity." He wanted his audience members to appreciate that this man had spoken out boldly when others demurred and that they too had a place in the story.

Despite potential calamity, President Davis said, "You must become your better self." He mesmerized the students as he urged them to step into their own. "How should you answer whenever the land is barren and the soul is in a wilderness?" Is it possible to cultivate "friendships or roses in the desert?"

"What," he asked, "are you to do?" Often, Prexy drew from the Old Testament and posed questions as though they were rhetorical. He provided his own answers as a recipe for social justice.

"As you play," he said paraphrasing Isaiah 35:1, "Consider it in your play. As you sing, let it reverberate in your song. As you think, think of the wilderness about and see if you can make it blossom into a rose."

The words rejected an angry cynicism in favor of a compassionate toughness. The plea to become one's "better self" in the face of adversity called individuals to respond to horrendous situations by turning unvoiced rage into courageous action. The words expected to find hope in the bleakest of moments. Do what you can to change things. Don't wallow in victimhood or revel in victory. Never use the excuse of tough times to ignore work to be done and do it, even if you are not the one benefitting. No excuses. You have power. When people begin to change, be transformed, care, then the land will heal and it will "blossom."

My father listened in the 1930s as President John W. Davis spoke. The men on the commuter train eighty years later never met my father, likely never heard Prexy or his story but the message rippled through the air and the ages. In a hard place, be a rose—petals, thorns and all. Summon courage from anger and make hope live.

A Collective Will

COMMUNICATING IN A meaningful way means going beyond what is superficial and getting to those things that matter. It requires a kind of multi-tasking: molding your own thoughts, hearing from others and considering how what you send and receive will have an impact beyond yourself. Ants do it best.

My first view of anthills in Dakar, Senegal, overwhelmed and humbled me beyond imagination. I've never forgotten what I saw from inside a station wagon rolling along a highway on the way to the ferry for historic Goree Island. The anthills were huge. Grandiose might be a better descriptor—seven, eight, ten feet tall or taller, standing so near to each other they could kiss. For a minute, I worried about the inhabitants, half expecting ants the size of people to emerge. The structures looked like an urban colony of mini skyscrapers spread across this semi-arid landscape. Little did I know at the time, that they, like icebergs, had more going on underground than above. The anthills I knew from my North Florida/South Georgia-red-clay childhood were minuscule. They were soft and easily destructible, no higher than an inch or two off the ground and scattered just enough to be a nuisance underfoot. But these were different.

I was in West Africa and everything seemed to be different from what I knew, although in a strange way, vaguely familiar. As we drove through the countryside, I saw dozens of dark brown earthen towers and did not know that these mini-mountains masked a subterranean megalopolis that rivaled the most elegant city constructed by humans. Little did I know that the ants themselves harbored a secret power that could be a model for life lessons.

Scientists say underground gardens and highways run through the ant colonies. I couldn't see that from where I sat in the car but what I saw impressed me. Even more remarkable is how these structures functioned and how they came to be. A single hill stood as evidence of endurance, divine sharing and a spirit of communal action. Together they looked like the product of a single mastermind. Our tour guide and friend told us that they were the collective will of a community. Dirt walls as thick and solid as cement and just as enduring stood witness.

To build, tiny ants actually hauled billions of loads of earth to the surface from underground, each ant carrying at least four times his own weight. But here's the kicker. Our guide told us it takes decades to build <u>one</u> of these anthills and the life expectancy of a single ant is seventy days!

How does that work? Ants may be designed to participate naturally in this ritual but what they do raises questions for all of us. How can anyone build an entity and, at the same time, teach another to keep the work going? How do you put together a structure knowing that you will never see it completed nor enjoy its benefits? How does one accept an assignment that doesn't seem related to the completion of the project? How do you find the strength and resilience to keep going when you can't even imagine the whole picture? How do you look beyond yourself and envision the end, doing your part at the beginning or in the middle? Why bother?

I considered it and drew a conclusion. You have to have enough love in you to want to do something big and enough courage in you to believe you can do what you never knew. You have to have enough grit in you to pull yourself up every day and enough trust in you to follow the lead of someone who is going before you. You have to have enough drive in you to push yourself beyond the limits of mediocrity and enough willingness in you to hand over something you can only carry so far. You have to have enough flexibility in you to change course when a change is needed and enough daring in you to pick up what someone else has dropped. You have to have enough humility in you to know you are not the center of it all, yet enough confidence to see that your role is critical.

And, most importantly, you have to believe in the divine order of things that has set you in place for the moment to do the work to further the conversation. Then you will see the world like an ant and do great things.

The Eyes Have It – Mahala and Sam

(Mahala Jackson and son Samuel – circa 1895)

"You are on the threshold of a new age.
Everything is possible; nothing is impossible."

–Oscar Moore
(an excerpt from a letter to the author, 1966)

T HE EYES FROM more than a century ago are the same. Dark, piercing, staring right through you as though they dare you to mess up, two sets of eyes watch from the photograph. They don't scream. They don't wail. They just look beyond a Birmingham, Alabama, that turned its back on a widowed colored mother with her son and toward a Cincinnati, Ohio, that held promise. More than the velvet that trims the dress or the leather gloves that cover the hands or the twenty buttons that close the bodice or the knickers and high boots, the eyes are what make you sit a little straighter when you see the photo, convinced you cannot be silent.

The photograph of my maternal great grandmother and my grandfather had watched me from the wall of my home in Tallahassee for a few years during my childhood. It had hung in the family room and served as a reminder that the world was not mine alone. My ancestors shared it. My mother had made a point of telling me some of their story—at least the parts she knew—in hopes that it would push me "to go farther and do more" than they had done.

Visitors noticing the photo often remarked that the "eyes ran in our family" and that the family resemblance was uncanny. Those eyes seemed to speak what they saw. They did not need words to convey the depth of pain, the height of commitment, nor the reach of pride they felt. They had marched past places that held no work and homes that had no shelter and people who offered no love. The eyes had tromped proudly into places where other people dared not go, but where these two sojourners proclaimed a space to be. From where they stood, the eyes looked back onto a past that limited direction for Negroes and toward a present that said, "Congratulations young Sam, on perfect attendance in Sunday School (1898)" at Allen Temple AME.

As a seamstress, Mahala worked for anyone who would pay a few coins for a garment. Her son Samuel became one of the first Negro letter carriers for the U.S. Postal Service in Cincinnati. Yet, the eyes bonded them by more than fabric and blood and mail runs to a line of people who claimed connections on two continents and working space on one. A perpetual "yes" embedded in their eyes blended her "mustard seed" faith, his pragmatic mind and the second sight of these two people who didn't know they had second sight.

The eyes looked into the future. They watched, what Samuel later called "a race trampled." They saw Black men lynched for some transgression against the social order, "crimes" the men were accused of committing in the promised land—robbery, looking at a white woman, mistaken identity, unruly remarks, throwing stones, smoking cigars. They saw Black women with bodies placed on display, limited in what they could study and who they could be. They saw disservice after disservice happen and they objected; they watched victory after victory occur and they applauded.

The eyes understood sports as a window on the world. Josh Gibson and Jackie Robinson had done diligence in the Negro Leagues so that Robinson (court martialed and pardoned in the Army) could play with the Brooklyn Dodgers so that when the team moved to Los Angeles Maury Wills could steal bases more than 50 times a season. All of this happened, Sam claimed, so that he could sit in the stadium when the Dodgers came to Cincinnati and cheer proudly as if his life depended on it. On another front, unnamed women played paddle tennis so that Ora Mae Washington could play court tennis (even when white women refused to play her) so that Althea Gibson could win Wimbledon. Although Sam never lived to see it, he would have boasted with no shame as he passed out cigars. He once watched Althea play and probably knew that she would one day lead to Venus and Serena Williams as they pirouetted on the promises made to them by another generation. The eyes imagined what would be.

The eyes of Mahala and Sam, frozen in time on celluloid, watched their descendants—four and five generations deep—stretch into institutions of higher learning, places of business, hallways of local and national government, theatre stages and screens of all sizes, carving out some place to be somebody. They figured out how to bring others along. They were determined to do everything in their power to snatch back anyone wandering and to rescue someone falling. In their permanent intensity, the eyes were relentless. They probed and pushed, grabbed hold and wouldn't let loose. They made room for the tiny and crowded out what was unsuited to be there in the first place. They held court and gave permission. At the same time, they did what they could to make sure no one in the family dropped out of the race.

When I look at the photograph, I see eyes that don't <u>hate</u> because they can't; eyes that don't <u>fear</u> because they don't know how; eyes that don't <u>cry</u> because it wouldn't matter. These are eyes that truly hope … and I'm thankful there is a family resemblance. I'm a witness.

Three Meditations on Being Six

"One day, I heard a piece of advice from someone who cared: 'Turn around and discover the world ...' "

—Anonymous

"That which God said to the rose, and caused it to laugh in full-blown beauty, He said to my heart, and made it a hundred times more beautiful."

—Julaluddin Rumi

Meditation #1: "Wings"

"WISH I HAD wings!" My 6-year-old granddaughter's declaration hung in the air. She speculated about angels and mermaids and which had the best life. Wings or tails? "Is it better to be in the air or in the water?" she asked, running on without waiting for an answer. Her innocence demanded more than a cursory response about worlds where neither air nor water should be feared but rather respected and seen as partners in possibilities.

She decided on her own that wings were better. She reasoned because of angels. Of all the things that angels can do—bring good news, announce grand things, guide wayward people, serve as intermediaries, guard heaven and earth—only one thing mattered to Makenzie. That they could fly! Like blue jays, they could soar. Like hummingbirds, they could hover. Like bees, they could be in one place in an instant and away from it all in a blink. For this little one, angels were real, their lives were complete, and their wings made it all happen. She would be better, she thought, if she had her own. I'm sure she was right.

Meditation #2: "On Being on the Page or Not"

I went into the children's section of a bookstore in early fall a few years ago to find a gift for a 6-year-old I know. There were no books there with Black people on the covers or in the titles, and the few that had Black faces in the stories were abysmal. The options jumping from the pages spoke to what was possible for other people. I thought about the 6-year-old I was shopping for and wondered if any of these books would give him a chance to find a place to breathe. Would they nurture his sense of self or would they crush his hope and make him feel like an outsider? Would they help define him as a decent human being or would they make him invisible and try to take away his humanity?

If you are 6 and you can't find yourself on the pages of a children's book, do you really exist? Or when you see yourself there, and you are only the "bad guy," does that matter? Even though there are bears and butterflies, caterpillars and creepy things in the book, you may feel excluded or erased if someone who looks like you is not among the faces of superheroes, smiling giants, the phalanx of people-characters who are good even while they have flaws. Or, you may feel you can't do anything when page after page lobs you images that cannot lift, sway, carry, move, sort, fix or change anything and _those_ are the images that look like you. You may be barely old enough to decipher words, but most likely you have enough years to recognize that there is a problem with the images.

A book can break or repair. It can help you understand and question what you know and what you don't. It literally can be a page-turner, a gut-shaker, a soul-stirrer, a future-maker. It can hook a heart and project a world. It can take you places you wish to be and bring you back from places you're happy to leave. It can show you people who can do great things and help you meet people who can breathe without restriction.

It can reaffirm who you are and make you feel good about who you want to be or it can destroy you with what's there or not there. Yet, in 2013, only 256 of the 3,200 children's books that were published were about people of color. By 2016, the numbers had improved slightly. In 2017, of the analyzed 3,700 total published children's books, 938 were about people of color.

Children's literature is supposed to build thinking skills, to help youngsters learn about themselves and the world. In reality, it can reinforce or undermine, teach accurately or mislead. It can help them deal with pain, joy, grief and difficult situations or tell them those emotions are not valid. Children are vulnerable and impressionable in the face of a story so it makes a difference what they read. We should want a variety of cultural perspectives radiating from books to help them have rich/deep conversations on the road to learning what it means to be human.

In early December, I finally found a gift book that would affirm my 6-year-old friend. I was attending a weekend holiday fair at Shiloh Baptist Church in Washington, D.C., when I found dozens of books, a real vendor's assortment piled high of heroes with good points and flaws. Stories of champions, past, present and future—imaginary and real—flooded the vendor's table like an avalanche. Books with visual and verbal messages diverse in ethnicity, gender, economic class were all there. I was in heaven as I leafed through the stash, delighted to know there were choices. Suddenly, I had an epiphany. These books had something magical for everyone. They offered the world a chance to see a child's possibilities. They gave my little friend a chance to recognize himself, to move to new places and to soar. The gift would have meaning. At 6 years old, my friend might even learn to love to read and the rest of his life would be different.

The author (center) at 6 years old at Lucy Moten Elementary School.
Then my name was "Judy" (with a "y")
but I could barely spell and could not read at all.

Meditation #3 - "Old Miss Seabrooks"

In 1954, I had no idea of the gravity of the year. I was 6 years old and attending an all Black school, not realizing the year would be a contested date, arm wrestled to the mat by educators on both sides of the racial divide. People shouted, "Change is coming to America" and either meant it, wished it or denied it. By May 1954, when the Supreme Court handed down its ruling in *Brown v. Board of Education*, I was starting first grade and had not yet learned to read. I was behind.

The school year dragged to a close and the next year I was in second grade at Lucy Moten Elementary School, named for the nineteenth century African American who had been a principal of Minor Teacher's College in Washington, D.C., and a physician who graduated from Howard University. Lucy Moten's fame as an educator had been embraced across the nation and many places in the South, like my elementary school, had been named in her honor. Most of our teachers were first rate, holding summer-earned graduate degrees from well-known northern universities that would admit Blacks. Armed with a missionary zeal, they taught us with hand-me-down textbooks that had raggedy pages and sometimes missing sections torn out by exuberant white students from schools across town. The books had come to us second hand; our facilities and equipment were previously used; and it was a fact, that I still could not read.

By this time, Miss Seabrooks had become my teacher. All of us called her "Old Miss Seabrooks" although she must have been no older than thirty. No-nonsense Ernestine Ford Seabrooks had a reputation for turning out students who did better than they imagined they could. She was a brilliant woman who had studied people. I was a talker, able to pull meaning from pictures—so I had extracted meaning from text-book stories by "reading" the pictures rather than the words. This had worked remarkably well but Old Miss Seabrooks saw right through it.

In class, I nervously took to becoming disruptive whenever the class began to read, performing my way through each day, trying to become the center of attention so that I could avoid tackling the written words. I talked more than I listened. Looking back, I believe this was clearly my defense and a ruse. The more my classmates read the texts and talked about what they read, the louder I became talking about anything else, trying my best in my childhood immaturity to distract them. And then one day as I proceeded to stir the pot with a side conversation, Old Miss Seabrooks stopped the class and turned squarely to me.

"Judy," she said with a look that took no prisoners, "Go sit in the corner." Stunned by the attention and the order, I complied and shuffled the few feet to the one chair—placed away from the twenty-six other kids—that gave me time to think.

Then Old Miss Seabrooks turned to the others and said, "Class, today we're going to learn a new word." They all waited in wide-eyed silence as she spoke.

"Repeat after me." The room was quiet.

"I-so-la-tion. Judy is in i-so-la-tion." Twenty-seven voices, mine included, repeated the new word and the sentence. "I-so-la-tion. Judy is in i-so-la-tion."

I was to stay there until I could participate in conversations with others without always selfishly insisting that we follow my agenda. Being in the corner for me was not about learning to fold, but rather preparing to be bold, to speak truth with a thoughtful honesty and to receive it the same way.

That was the first and only time I sat in the corner publicly shamed on the surface but changed inside. Never did I have to return. While the incident did not make me a big fan of Old Miss Seabrooks, it motivated me to listen. It taught me that conversations were more than just talking. I found myself paying attention. The by-product? Begrudgingly, I learned to read.

When I complained to my Mom about "Old Miss Seabrooks" and her way of doing things, Mama made it plain.

"Sometimes," she said in her infinite wisdom, "We learn in spite of the teacher not because of the teacher."

I never quite knew if this teacher had committed herself to every child in her class, or if she had ever made a sacred promise to prepare every girl and boy for a future that didn't want them. I never knew if she understood what ultimately would happen to those who were both illiterate and Black and, therefore, outside the possibilities she could only imagine. I never knew if she realized that any of her students who couldn't read might someday be at the mercy of a system where words ruled. Did she know that without the right skills, conversations would be narrow and so would individuals? Did she understand how reading can deepen our awareness of what's going on and extend our thoughts? I never could be certain of any of this. But I do know that I jumped ahead in reading that year and stayed at least three grade levels ahead for the next 10 years. I know that I didn't claim I was doing it for "Old Miss Seabrooks," but I did it because I really did not want to live life in isolation.

Calvin Bess' Footstep

"Stories live forever, but storytellers don't.
Listen to the foot soldiers while you can."

–Patricia Stephens Due

August 13, 2016

I STOOD AND STARED at the footprint and couldn't help but travel back 50 years. Calvin Bess. The name reminded me that time had passed but hurts remained. In uptown Tallahassee, the footprint lay wedged between the historic Florida State Capitol building that for me had once housed humiliating contempt and the back door of the old McCrory's where lunch counter protesters had taken their seats and refused to budge. The five and dime had been the site of confrontations two miles from my high school. Now the Civil Rights path outside the defunct McCrory's door served as a memorial for giants. The sidewalk was new, but the story was not. In 2016, this one block long sidewalk honored and remembered the "foot soldiers" of the Movement who had shouted "Jail, no bail" when arrested for wanting to sit and eat with some modicum of dignity. It honored those in Tallahassee's bus boycott and others who had done much more.

I had come home to Tallahassee for my fiftieth high school reunion. Twenty-eight Baby Rattlers from our forty-eight member class of 1966 had returned to reminisce and recall candy apples and boiled peanuts; the days of football games, home economics and science labs; the disappointments and dreams of another time when we were young and wide-eyed and expectant. We had lived through an era that had wrapped us in prom dust and covered us with blood tears all at the same time. Some had been a part of the Movement, joining the Student Nonviolent Coordinating Committee (SNCC) and the Congress of Racial Equality (CORE) and a host of other revolutionary groups that had names they could clearly remember and that positioned them to do things they would never forget. The 1960s had been tough but our classmates from little FAMU High had been tougher. Following graduation, some of us had gone to work, others to more schools, still others did both— becoming a state legislator, a physician, a nurse, an entrepreneur, a journalist, a librarian, a high school coach, a producer/director, a contractor, a military officer, artists, college professors, scholars, government administrators and workers, corporate CEOs, administrative coordinators, parents, grandparents and good citizens. Many of us had made history as we moved beyond the confines of the city to other places. We had taken literally the growing-up messages from our teachers—that our lives were worth nothing unless we put them on the line. In different ways we had lived that code.

On a ninety-five degree day dripping with characteristic North Florida humidity, a handful of us—greyed, sweating and anxious— mounted a tour bus and rode through the city, visiting places that held many memories. As the bus stopped on East Jefferson near the corner of Monroe, we piled out. For the first time, I thought about the contradictions embedded in the names of the streets at that intersection. Monroe and Jefferson—two U.S. presidents. James Monroe had bought Florida from Spain in another century and Thomas Jefferson, author of the Declaration of Independence, had been grandfather to the man who began the then all-white Florida State University a few blocks down the street. They were two of the "Founding Fathers" of our democracy. Both had been slaveholders.

There in 2016, at the intersection of the streets were footprints of foot soldiers on the ground. One stood out. His full name had been George Calvin Bess, Jr., but everyone who knew him had called him Calvin.

Here it was, the name memorialized in concrete on a sidewalk that stretched for a block and ripped into every passing heart that bothered to stop and remember or learn the story for the first time.

Calvin Bess had been a Baby Rattler too. He was not in our class but was one of the "big boys" we looked up to in our segregated demonstration school that had some four hundred students in grades 1 through 12. Those of us who had been together since first grade, remembered Calvin, about four years ahead of us, for his freckles and his reddish complexion. My mother had been his homeroom teacher and had called him "a quiet boy" from a modest family. Yet Calvin had always refused to be silent when he saw something wrong. In fact, a later account of his life recalled the time when Calvin, while still a student in training to be an activist, accompanied another SNCC member to a rural Black church service. When the pastor refused to allow the SNCC member to speak to the congregation, Calvin—unsolicited— yelled out without permission, insisting to the congregation that they must register to vote.

The right to vote was his passion. He had seen people in Northern Florida denied this basic right and forced to live with the consequences of poor representation. He had seen outrageous literacy tests and $2 poll taxes as part of a system that gave voting privileges to whites and denied them to Blacks. For the men and women of the South who deserved better, in 1967, Calvin headed off to Mississippi in a shiny blue convertible his Daddy had given him. At 22 and about to graduate college, he joined a host of other courageous students from across the country who travelled on a mission. Among them were many whites who were allies in the fight. Working all along the way, Calvin drove from Tallahassee through neighboring Gadsden County where there were more than twelve thousand Blacks eligible to vote and just a few years before had only seven Blacks who were actually registered.

We don't know for certain what happened when he reached Mississippi, but likely he began to knock on doors, confronting individual fears of people who never thought they would have a chance. There had been no poplar trees "with Black bodies swinging in the breeze" as in Billie Holiday's *Strange Fruit*, but there had been danger and he had found it. Citizens wanted to vote. Calvin believed they had the right to do it, but forces in the universe converged to try to quiet his voice. It is likely that he faced the KKK, the police and state officials (sometimes who were one in the same). Mysteriously, he disappeared and days later, his blue convertible—charred and no longer shiny—was found at the bottom of a swamp. He was in it with a hole in his head.

The family took it the hardest, never knowing what actually happened. Calvin's baby sister who was 6 years old when he died kept looking for the fellow she called "Brother" to come home. Calvin's mother never got over the tragedy and eventually passed away, perhaps of a broken heart. Calvin's dad, in the aftermath of his son's death, insisted that the burned-out blue convertible be brought back to Tallahassee for all to see. Neighbors say that car sat in the Bess' front yard for nearly six months as a reminder of the high price the son had paid. Three years before, three other Civil Rights workers—Michael Schwerner, Andrew Goodman and James Chaney— had been viciously murdered for doing the same work. They had become a part of the national conversation. Calvin Bess never did, but he left something to follow anyhow.

Those of us Baby Rattlers looking at the footprint on the Civil Rights memorial sidewalk were the survivors. We were the ones, who by the Grace of God, were still here. Others like Calvin, because of somebody else's bigotry and hatred and fear, never made it. At that moment, I was convinced the imprint in the sidewalk meant more than just the concrete used to create it, more than the historical record used to resurrect it, more than the sprinkles of dirt that now blew from the Tallahassee street intersection of contractions. In that footprint lay hope and a real expectation that the inanimate footprint could become a living footstep. We could be better Americans. If we told someone this story and let it lead us, it could be an example of justice and tolerance to follow. We could give up our complacency and indifference and excuses. We could make sure there never came an election we would "sit out" or "miss." We could be certain we raised our voices and pushed our resolve so that every eligible person we knew voted—if not for our own sake and the sake of our progeny, for the sake of Calvin Bess. I realized he would expect it and we could do it.

When Mom Talked
With Her Toes

"Hope ... permits a person to live his life on his own terms. It is part of the human spirit to heal and give a miracle a chance to happen."

> –Jerome Groopman, M.D.
> *The Anatomy of Hope*

CONVERSATIONS HAPPEN WHEN you're open to join them. My mother always had something to say whether anyone asked her opinion or not. She spent days making sure her student teachers from the College of Education at Florida A&M University, stationed around the state were prepared to be the vanguard of a generation of Black high school teachers. They needed to know how to engage and exchange. The 1960s were pinching them tight, not welcoming them to work but Mom could see that one day, things would be different. At home in Tallahassee, she continued to listen and encourage, frequently offering advice to students, filling them with common sense wisdom. And she was usually right. Even when people didn't ask her opinion, she gave it and she listened: at Non-Parrell's Bridge Club meetings, at PTA meetings for Lucy Moten Elementary, at vestry meetings for St. Michael's and All Angels, or anywhere.

So, when she developed pneumonia and we put her in the hospital at midyear of 2007, we thought she had slowed down, that her conversations had been curtailed with her health. It was a shock. She had moved to the Washington, D.C., metropolitan area to live with us and we hadn't expected her to be sick even though she was just three months shy of her ninetieth birthday. Except for the osteoporosis that bent her nearly in two, up until that time, she had been in pretty fair health. But then on a day after returning from a vacation in St. Thomas, her color changed, her skin began to droop and she began a downward spiral. Rapidly deteriorating, she wilted. The doctors on her medical team at Howard University put her in intensive care and we were anxious.

The pneumonia fluctuated and then one day, out of nowhere, she rallied. Not sure why, but she did. She sat up in the bed as if she were ready to "hold court" and began offering her opinion on just about everything. The doctors moved her to a regular room. Just short of giving autographs, she became the hit of the hospital, entertaining a parade of visitors who came to wish her well and, at the same time, get a dose of her wisdom.

June 21. Mom took another turn and had to go back to ICU. My girlfriends Effie and Mel claimed to be her "other daughters" as they boldly entered the ICU where only family could visit. It was Mom's birthday and they were determined to be there. "Two at a time" was the rule the ICU nurse reminded us to follow. Every day for the next few weeks my friends made it clear that they should be there since they were members of the "family." Other members of her extended family came too and claimed to be relatives. Tootie and Paula, Brenda and Don, Jean and Marilyn, who Mom had nicknamed her "twins" even though they looked nothing alike and were not even related to each other. Also visiting were medical students who, in this teaching hospital, were practicing for their futures.

Whenever student trainees entered, Mom perked up and immediately switched into her academic mode becoming the consummate teacher—probing, encouraging, forgetting about herself. "What year are you?" she wanted to know of the fellow who came to check her blood pressure. "What is your major?" she asked the woman taking her other vitals. "How's the class work coming?" she queried the night nurse fully expecting to get a response and participate. Always eager for a conversation, she dispensed tidbits, listened to woes, and urged soon-to-be graduates to think of their training beyond themselves.

One day in July her breathing became more labored than usual and the nurses on duty intubated her and added a respirator. They closed the curtain and took only a few minutes to insert the flexible plastic tube into her trachea. When they pulled back the curtain, the same apparatus that made her breathing easier made me gasp to see it. My precious Mom, a fiercely independent woman, now lay hooked to the hospital wall and to a pole with tubes running everywhere. She was declining. Completely dependent on someone to turn her, to speak for her, she appeared helpless even though her eyes still danced.

I sat with her completely silent for two days, wrapped in my own fears. Then early afternoon on the third day, I heard behind me a disembodied voice. "Shall we proceed with the process?" A petite respiratory therapist entered the room raising the question. She had been there tentatively, at least twice before, earlier in the day. But at this hour she seemed to march in boldly with a team of others, coming out of nowhere. I sat at the side of Mom's bed taking it all in. "The process" she referred to was a protocol involving a series of treatments ending with the removal of the intubation tube. The doctor in the waiting room earlier had described the process as having worked in a few similar cases. The chances, he said, were 50/50 that she could breathe on her own once the tube was removed. The outcome was, however, uncertain. It took a moment for me to realize that the time I had dreaded had arrived.

Although Mom's living will did not explicitly describe the process, that document gave me—her only child, daughter of her heart, the sole surviving Moore—the Power of Attorney to make decisions on her behalf. It clearly designated me to speak for her, "… in the event that" she had been "determined to be incapable of providing informed consent for medical treatment." I was fully grown with children and even grandchildren, but I wasn't ready for this.

Dr. Robert Williams could feel my angst. He was an extraordinary man, a gentle physician with a bedside manner that exuded compassion and demanded you to come along with him to find it. I pulled him aside and told him my dilemma: how much guilt I felt, how conflicted I was in the face of such a life and death decision; how

I really didn't want to make the decision I was compelled on paper to make. He responded simply by asking one question: "What does your Mom want?"

I looked at him as though he had completely lost it. Could he really mean the question? Certainly, he knew better than I that she couldn't talk. With tubes everywhere, she couldn't give one of her classic well-crafted responses full of reasoning and absolute truth. Surely he could see this.

"I don't know." My answer was clear and plain and abrupt, full of my hidden impatience that silently screamed, "Can't you see what I see?"

A beat and he said, "Why don't you ask her?"

And without waiting for me to obey what I thought was a ridiculous directive, he walked to Mom's side and with all the respect of having a conversation with someone on equal ground, he looked her directly in the eyes.

"Mrs. Moore, if you can hear me, wiggle your toes." Mom's toes began moving vigorously back and forth with a passion I recognized. "If you'd like to communicate this way," he continued, "wiggle the toes on your left foot." The left toes moved and so did my heart.

It had never occurred to me to ask her anything in this state. Rather, I made the assumption that people usually make when they think others have nothing to say. They fail to engage; they miss the opportunity to exchange.

"Wiggle your toes." It was a directive that was liberating for Mom and for me. It opened a whole new way of communicating. I explained to Mom the process that the medical team had shared with me, including the benefits and the dangers. I explained it all very meticulously, being careful not to omit a thing. After I asked if she understood, I asked her what she wanted to do. She made the decision. I was relieved.

Someone might say the decision was the wrong one. Mom died seven days later. But who knows, it may have been that her decision gave her seven days to prepare me for what was ahead. Seven is the Biblical number of completion or wholeness. During those seven days, we talked about having enough faith to believe, about having enough curiosity to wonder, about having enough courage to move on. We talked with a new language: I listened with my heart and speculated and she wiggled her toes and spoke no words. She had something more to say and I was grateful I could hear it.

After the tubes were removed, I never took for granted a single breath Mom breathed. I knew the precious moments counted. Near the end, she wiggled her toes, took off her oxygen mask herself and with the breath she could muster, three times she quickly said, "I love you, I love you, I love you!" I reasoned she said it one time for God; one time for Dad who she was about to rejoin; and one time for me. But it was the wiggle of her toes that reassured me most, gave me comfort, told me that all this was part of God's divine plan. It was the wiggle of the toes that showed me how to have a conversation, even when words were not there.

My Mom was a rose and to the end, she continued to teach beyond herself. I'm grateful.

And There Was One

"Silence is the enemy of history, and history is all we have."

–Daniel Black,
The Coming

P EOPLE TOLD ME that it wouldn't be easy. Those who had gone before said it might take at least one or two hours just to navigate the first floor and then you weren't guaranteed to see everything. But, they shared, it was worth it. You needed at least two visits and probably many more before you realized how much you were changed as a result. An incredible history of lived lives, shared communities, broken promises, captured hopes, precious memories and sacred fragments lay collected in the new National Museum of African American History and Culture on the National Mall in Washington, D.C. An engineering, architectural and technological feat offered a testament to a people's resilience. It was amazing.

When I found myself among the excited visitors at the Smithsonian's newest Museum two months after it opened 2016, I was overwhelmed. So much of the story I thought I knew was tumbling out in new layers too deep to explore at one time.

Of all of the things I saw, of all the artifacts and photographs displayed in interactive exhibits, of all the images and sounds bombarding the senses, of all the texts available to read, one line had the biggest impact on me. One wall entry stopped me short in my tracks. One text made it almost impossible to go on. As I walked into the alcove that held the story of the horrific Middle Passage where millions of enslaved people had been brutalized while being transported to the Americas, I saw it—although not at first. As part of the wallpaper, it blended inconspicuously with the dark shadow of the abyss and made no claim to being profound. Hundreds of similar entries formed a mosaic that made it almost impossible to see. In fact, I missed it the very first time I was in the room and my friend who had been before to the museum insisted on bringing me back to the room to see it. I needed to be a witness. Entries on the wall served as background and actually meant something. Each had its own truth embedded in it. Each was the result of meticulous research. Each had a responsibility attached to it.

Mapped on the walls was a record of a wretched course, offering as close as we can get today to those who were there. There were entries by name of the slave ship, the country owning the ship, the date it left West Africa, the number of enslaved who were boarded and the number of enslaved who survived. Hundreds of such entries on the walls each had its own hidden story. But one struck me.

Ship Name	Country	Voyage Began	Enslaved Boarded/Survived
SAINT MICHEL	France	12-10-1730	170/1

The *Saint Michel*. On this French vessel, one hundred and seventy enslaved people left West Africa against their will, ripped from families and homeland. Squeezed into the dank hole of the ship in a space with barely eighteen inches between them, they lay chained, forced to eat, sleep, defecate, urinate, menstruate, give birth, vomit and exist together for ninety days, one hundred and twenty days, or more. They didn't know where they were going, what lay ahead, or if they would ever return home. They must have seen their fellow enslaved men and women leap overboard when brought from the ship's bottom for air, be raped as they experienced the worst humiliation imaginable, and die from what was unimaginable. They must have endured force-feeding and must have felt abject violations of their diseased bodies. They must have touched each other through their chains willingly and not, as they tried desperately to hold onto their minds and cried out to their God for relief of their spirits. One hundred seventy of them left the port on the ship. One survived.

Who was that one? How did he or she make it through? What resolve or promise or spoken word or sacred will made it possible to be the one? What happened to this survivor? Was he or she ever able to step beyond the chains and see himself again? What of progeny? Were there any? Was I it?

One got off that ship alive and I could be the descendent. I could be the one brought/left here to tell the story of the stench and the tears, of the beauty and the dark pride, of the history and the hope. I stood there for a moment and realized I was a miracle. Imagine, if I am a descendant of that <u>one</u> or of any of the "ones" on that wall, I need to thank God. I have an obligation to speak.

If It Happened Once
on Robben Island ...

*"History, despite its wrenching pain, cannot be unlived,
but if faced with courage, need not be lived again."*

–Maya Angelou
"On the Pulse of Morning"

I N 1985, I never imagined going to South Africa. In fact, I vowed I
never would. The hatred generated by the humiliation of one group
and systematic elevation of another had ripped apart that country.
Legal racial divisions were ugly; the brutal regime of Pieter Botha was
vicious; the minority rule by whites oppressed the majority population;
and the world thought of the country as a pariah. In the United States, a
protest movement had emerged, led by TransAfrica's Randall Robinson,
Civil Rights Commissioner Mary Frances Berry; law professor Eleanor
Holmes Norton, and D.C. Congressman Walter Fauntroy. Grassroots
community groups like the Southern Africa Support Project (SASP)
gave political and material assistance.

The least I could do, I felt, was to dig in my heels on this side of the
world to support the anti-apartheid *Free South Africa Movement*, using
every resource I had, including my body. I joined daily marches, signed
petitions, boycotted businesses that economically supported apartheid
and even volunteered with dozens of other protesters to be arrested at
the South African embassy on Massachusetts Avenue in Washington,
D.C.

Then, in 1990 a string of political changes unraveling apartheid
made me think differently about wanting to go to South Africa. First

the decades-old ban on the anti-apartheid African National Congress (ANC) was lifted. Then the country released Nelson Mandela—freedom fighter, hero of the movement and head of the ANC. For twenty-seven years, Mandela had been imprisoned by the illegal South African government. Eighteen of those years he spent on desolate Robben Island, isolated from family and the people he was bound one day to lead. When Mandela walked free from prison in February 1990, he carried a new national hope with him. He participated in the negotiated end to apartheid and remarkably four years later, when an unprecedented democratic election allowed all South Africans to vote, Mandela was elected president.

Within a decade of Mandela's rise, I visited South Africa in 1999, and my eyes opened, not because of something big but because of something possible. I saw a new perspective on struggle and conversations.

A short ferry ride took us from pristine Cape Town to Robben Island, the once-prison that had become a museum, complete with historic wall signs offering the narrative nightmare so many had lived. The 8 x 7-foot cells remained as they had been—sparse, cold and devoid of anything resembling humanity. Cells were preserved for decades with only a straw mat, flimsy blanket and tiny eye-level window for peering out. The names of famous former prisoners Walter Sisulu, Govan Mbeki, and others were on the walls. As a place for tourists, the prison had a strange unnerving effect.

"Welcome to Robben Island!"

The voices of docents in unison caught me off guard as we entered the prison gates. When Mandela had arrived in 1964, he heard a different greeting—one all political prisoners received when they came: "This is the Island," an armed guard had barked, fortified by a German Shepherd. "Here you will die!" History said that only two prisoners had ever escaped the Island since it had become a prison and before that, in the nineteenth century, as a leper colony, had offered another kind of death sentence.

On the day we visited, a former prisoner and a former prison guard showed us the place together. One Black and one white. Our docents spoke not just as trained storytellers but as people who had been actual players in the real-life drama. One had been prisoner for two decades living in the same cellblock as Mandela— Block B reserved for those considered most politically dangerous. The other docent had been the jailer or warder. The two told about the stagnant conditions for Blacks and "coloreds" imprisoned there: how prisoners daily emptied their toilet buckets and did hard labor with automatic weapons trained on them; how they toiled in the nearby lime rock quarry and watched their health deteriorate.

In measured and detailed interlocking stories our tour guides helped us "see" the torture those prisoners experienced, and the high walls intended to block their communication with other prisoners. They seemed to talk to each other, not just to us. One would start a story and the other might finish it. The docents showed us the yard, the warden's office and the area for solitary confinement, making sure we understood that prisoners could only receive one letter every six months. One guide told us the extraordinary lengths to which super-vising powers went, trying to prevent contact among inmates. The other guide explained the ingenious lengths prisoners went to maintain that contact with each other.

The white tour guide helped us "feel" what it was like to restrict the reading materials of prisoners—letters, books, articles, anything thought to bring the outside world in. He told of how he and his fellow white guards doled out humiliation, forcing political prisoners naked and strip-searching them in the courtyard.

The Black tour guide helped us understand how those same prisoners endured and circumvented such ritual indignities. When they complained about the damp cells and were told their bodies would absorb the moisture, they steeled themselves against the dampness. When they were forbidden to speak by a warder who patrolled the long corridor of their cellblock all night long, they sprinkled sand on the ground to be able to hear his approach so they might hush their defiant whispers before he reached them. Vivid and clear, the picture emerged of lives that moved across decades behind bars but not devoid of hope. The stories were a reminder that those who thought themselves powerful could never snuff out the resistance nor silence those who had an obligation to speak.

I heard a lot and saw even more. After one hour of tracing steps of apartheid that political prisoners on Robben Island had lived for years, our group of tourists reached the open dining area and the end of our formal tour. We dispersed, individually contemplating the unimaginable. I noticed the Black docent off to the side sitting on one of the original well-worn wall benches. I wondered about him as a person, as a human being reconciling his work with his life. How did he do this day after day? I decided to join him on the stone bench that had no doubt heard many whispered secrets.

"How do you work beside someone who treated you like an animal for two decades?" I asked. It was a question that came from deep in my soul. I really wanted to know about how you turn the corner when you've always seen someone as the enemy and you know they see you as the same.

"How can you repeat these stories to tourists with your jailer?" I said the words out loud. There had been so much hatred, so many angry expressions during apartheid, so much division that had ripped apart the body and spirit. I couldn't imagine reliving it, especially in the company of one who perpetuated it.

"How can you do it?" I asked again.

With the absolute firmness of his conviction and from deep within his humanity, the Black docent looked me square in the eye. Without blinking, he answered. "We are called to forgive."

His genuine sincerity humbled me and reminded me of my own responsibility. As much as my Christian upbringing had taught that very thing, my daily living had challenged me to forget it. As much as I knew that one shouldn't "hate the person" but rather "hate the injustice," things I had seen happening around me made me want to do otherwise. But the guide's statement echoed in my head. "We're called to forgive." And then, as I sat, he added. "It's a place to start."

Some would argue that forgiveness is a cop out, a way of avoiding action, an excuse for not taking charge. But embedded in the tour guide's words was something much bigger. He was suggesting that forgiveness can be a beginning point for a conversation. It would not replace self-love; nor would it exchange passivity for action to mitigate a wrong; it would not substitute for correction; nor would it supplant an egregious offense. Indeed, it was necessary to acknowledge that the wrong had happened. Forgiveness is not intended to mean that individuals sit idly by, refusing to push an injustice closer to its resolution nor its perpetrator closer to his consequences. But, rather, forgiveness is intended to open a door to talk and to understand another's point of view.

The Black tour guide had said, "We are called to forgive," but I wondered if the other docent felt the same way. Did he feel or want forgiveness? Could he forgive himself? If I could have found him before we left, I would have asked. He may have told me, like other white South Africans later showed me and like former jailers told Mandela after his release: "We would rather forget."

Forgetting seemed to be an antidote for many white South Africans who saw conversations about race and historic separations as tough. Forgetting, they implied, must be superior to forgiving. Certainly, it did not require courage, nor did it require a conscience to be activated. It did not require soul-searching nor self-reflection about the nightmare that had occurred. It seemed to be an easy way out.

But the white docent I met on Robben Island had not chosen to go this route. He had not forgotten. Rather, he had engaged in telling hard stories that demanded confrontation. He had elected to tell of what Mandela called "stamping out the spark that makes each of us human." He had chosen to reveal his complicity in that experiment. That took courage.

In the days following apartheid, South Africa assembled a Truth and Reconciliation Commission designed, as it claimed, to help the country "come to terms with the …past on a morally accepted basis." Hundreds of South Africans, victims and perpetuators of oppression, responded and participated, seeing themselves on the edge of hope.

On Robben Island on the day I visited, I saw a glimmer of hope. In this corner of the country, people with divisions were not ignoring them. They were sharing stories from different vantage points and in a tiny way were beginning to face their animosities and fears, speaking without malice, guilt or shame. Who knows what would happen when land and property were reallocated and jobs and other resources were redistributed? But at that moment, at least, before any felt their security threatened, they were beginning.

That day I learned something about conversations if they are to take place: they should be rooted in a real desire to have them; they should be truthful and respectful; they should acknowledge the hidden stories that arise on both sides between human equals; and they should honor the disservice that has been done anywhere it exists. It is imperative!

Part III:

Toward a Conversation

"The cause of freedom is not the cause of a race or a sect, a party or a class – it is the cause of humankind, the very birthright of humanity."

–Anna Julia Cooper

"But in terms of how we talk, we have got to understand our interconnectedness ... We're at a place in history when we need a conversation..."

–William J. Barber II

A Tool Kit: A Story-Hope Primer

"Ubuntu: I am because of you…"

—Desmond Tutu

A Word about *Ubuntu*: Toward a Conversation

THE UNIFYING SPIRIT of "Ubuntu," which grew out of the South African journey to nationhood, suggests that you can't be human all by yourself. We all have an innate interdependency that is vital to our being. The philosophy posits that with interconnectedness comes responsibility. If we are to be truly human then, we must not only know our own stories but also learn others' stories. Knowing only one side gives us a false sense of the world. As the writer Chimamanda Ngozi Adichie tells us: "It is morally urgent to have honest conversations."

It is difficult to live in a place bruised by divisions without believing it can be better, without expecting that one day things will change. For millions who hope, there is a promise to restore truth even in the United States where that concept has eroded.

Landmark events rooted in race have shaped our national identity for as long as the nation has existed. Now in this complex 21st century, raw emotions, deep-seated fears—as well as anxieties once buried and seldom discussed—have resurfaced. At the center are congealed and hardened assumptions about "racial others" that drive wedges and fuel bigotry. We are at each other's throats with vitriol that is brazen and toxic. We sling racial slurs like snowballs. We have been socialized not to talk about race and we have been taught that race is a real thing, when, in fact, it is something human beings have made up to describe our superficial differences. Few candid and revealing conversations occur across the so-called "racial divide." That must change. Our own personal stories are a beginning.

How do you bridge a chasm that seems un-crossable? What do you do when civility flees, the indictments fly and the discussion becomes a vulgar shouting match? How can people engaged in a conversation maintain their own identities and respect the identities of others? How do you address serious moral issues that have been overlooked or issues of social justice that have been denied? These questions are tough but stories may offer keys to the answers.

Everybody craves stories. Since the beginning of humankind, narratives packed with emotional depth have pushed individuals to action and cohesion or inaction and separation. They reveal more uncomfortable truths than mere facts. Imagine moving toward *Ubuntu* by using the powerful possibilities of what might be called Story-Hope to build our bigger clan—our human family.

This book is designed to show the power of Story-Hope, the power of the personal narrative to promote discussions and build bridges. Here are a few assumptions undergirding the book:

- Racial designations come with accumulated advantages and disadvantages.

- We unconsciously fear others.

- Matters of race, gender and class are potentially divisive.

- Apologies are not overrated; neither is forgiveness.

- Unintentional racism is alive and well.

- Given the right tools and the right stories, people engaging in conversations can move toward reconciliation.

A Word about Using the Tool Kit: Toward the Work of Real Talk

This Tool Kit section offers guidance on using Story-Hope—a reconciliation method allowing individuals to draw on their own personal stories and recollections to step into their discomfort and engage others in tough yet honest conversations. Best done face-to-face in person, the conversations must happen. The ultimate goals are to end divisiveness between, among and within groups that consider each other "other"; to acknowledge exploitive and oppressive behavior; and to move toward a sympathetic and mutual understanding.

Regardless of an individual's point of view—centered or marginalized, ignored or acknowledged—the idea is to connect through open and honest dialogue. Such dialogue about racial matters is difficult for many reasons, chief among them are these three:

- <u>Fear</u> - We are afraid of being misunderstood or labeled "racist" or "victim" if we speak honestly. We have unspoken anxiety that revealing our brokenness may make us vulnerable. We also fear shifts in power, the unknown and the unfamiliar. We are reluctant to confront change.

- <u>Failure</u> - We fail to acknowledge our own shortcomings and prejudices. In addition, we fail to act on what we really know.

- <u>Intractable attitudes</u> - Even in the face of strong evidence contradicting what we believe and know to be true, we hold on to those stereotypes about others that we have learned and that are confirmed by media. We take mental short cuts and make assumptions. We refuse to budge.

Research shows that if we can find ways to address fears, failures and long-held traditional biases, we can shift attitudes.

Sometimes there is a need for intra-racial dialogue to root up and root out class or color-based cankers lingering and festering. In these situations, the same reality is true. Individuals must come empathetically into conversations wanting to understand and to heal.

A Few Steps to Advance a Conversation

Here are ideas of how to begin.

- <u>Try one-on-one encounters</u>: These may be chance impromptu or planned conversations at work, in school, at places of worship, during leisure time, in the neighborhood or elsewhere at other times. Places considered sacred and safe are best. Be open to the opportunity to talk and listen whenever an appropriate situation arises. Be willing to take the initiative to begin and have the courage to follow through. Be respectful of each perspective.

- <u>Establish a Story-Hope Circle</u>: This is a small group set up for the express purpose of sharing stories across a racial divide. Co-workers, fellow students, neighbors, friends or acquaintances from other venues mutually decide to form such a group that meets once, periodically or on a recurring basis. Any three people or more may become a "Story-Hope Circle" and the group might ideally become no larger than ten. (A manageable-sized group encourages honest exchanges among members.) Length of time, frequency of gathering, format of meeting and venue should all be flexible and determined by what works for the individuals involved. Members of the Story-Hope Circles should share the following principles and/ or actions:

  o Each group will plan its gathering format. One facilitator/ story starter will throw out questions or tell a story to initiate conversation.

  o The group may use <u>one story</u> with candid information that has an emotional "hook" as a conversation starter. For example, a story about an encounter with a Confederate flag or a police officer or a noose hanging in a prominent place might be a catalyst for discussion. Or, a story about a perceived slight, an insult hurled or one received might encourage other stories. Other stories might emerge from remembering people who have taught you something you believe is significant. Consider the following when deciding upon an opening story: Does what happened make a difference? Will anybody be changed as a result?

- <u>Participate in a town hall style conversation on race</u>: Find the courage to work with local public officials and/or private nonprofits to establish conversations. Look for partnerships with local public schools and community organizations already engaged in discussions. If such do not yet exist, create them. Consider ways to moderate the stories.

- <u>Have online discussions</u>: Social media conversations offer unique opportunities. A photo widely shared could be a discussion-starter for a single issue, since a selected image can go beyond words and get to the heart of a particular perspective. Be advised though that the digital space, unlike any other, can be a place where tough issues are raised but also where big challenges occur. Questions of identity, security and veracity arise as issues of cyber warfare surface and threaten to disrupt honest conversations. Social media formats can have other limitations and challenges.

  o As evidenced by a U.S. President who fueled racial animosities with tweets, discussions online can get out of hand.

  o Fake identities—online disguises—provided by social media have emboldened individuals to go on the attack against others or to hide vitriol behind pretense. Even when identities are not hidden, social media may encourage gross misstatements.

  o In addition, some photo messaging and mobile applications are auto deleted and gone forever once they are read—making it difficult to maintain a sustained exchange of ideas. Others have limited space (i.e. Twitter's 280 characters).

The path from words to actions is direct and powerful and must be considered with caution. While online storytelling may be convenient and easy, it is not as effective as interpersonal face-to-face storytelling in the long term.

The key is to start. What's at stake is our humanity. This Tool Kit is designed to support and facilitate conversations with worksheets and interactive activities offering starter suggestions and tips for anyone interested.

Recommended Techniques

Recommendation #1 - Prepare your story

- Know your story and be willing to share it.

- Be genuine.

- Tell the truth. Remember, your story can be a point of departure, a rallying point and a tool to move forward.

- Ask yourself: "What is the story about me I am trying to tell?" "What is the story about the world I am trying to tell?" "Why is it important?"

- Recall and do an inventory of your life experiences. Choose those experiences that resonate with you for one reason or another. Think about the way they made you feel. As you recall them, try not to censor them.

- Consider the conflict, drama and lessons learned from an experience. Consider a plot line.

- Give yourself permission to remember. Think about the difficult and the easy, the painful and the pleasant, the memorable and the moving. All of this has the potential to provide material for good stories.

- Create vivid pictures by drawing clear mental images. Think of examples that provide sensory evidence—smells, sounds, sights, tactile experiences that vividly capture the moments you remember. Fit these into your stories.

- Remember… Your story matters.

Recommendation #2 - Prepare yourself

- Respect yourself. Love your story. Embrace your beauty and your narrative.

- Start with your own personal biases/prejudices. Tell the truth.

  o Look at what you consider "disposable lives" and know that there really are none. Every life has value and is worthy of respect.

  o Dismiss your assumptions about anyone you consider different from you. Make a conscious effort to face your prejudices from the start.

  o Think about what you have "decided already" about the other person. Take time to really "see" things from another point of view.

  o Know that there is a difference between intent and impact. You may have honorable intentions but your actions may have a negative impact.

- Have radical empathy. Ordinary empathy is too small for what is needed in the face of what is at stake. Radical, in this case, means a new thing, not the same old way of feeling but rather a completely new way driven by a new wind. Remember that you have a real capacity to feel. Radical empathy is different from ordinary empathy in that it requires feeling the urgency of someone else's freedom. It means being completely convinced— to the depths of your being—that freedom is necessary and unequivocal. This kind of empathy is different from sympathy, which requires you to look up or down. Radical empathy requires you to look across in a way that is more than simply casual so that you see someone else really as you would see yourself. Understand that there is only one human species and the goal is to become invested in another person's life beyond a neutral stance so that you think ethically about who your neighbor is.

Recommendation #3 — Tell your story

- Find your voice and use it.
- Take bold initiative. Be the first to start the conversation.
  - o Be willing to expose yourself and your shortcomings.
  - o Realize that sometimes one's starting point is another's endpoint. What one person has just learned may be what the other person has known all along.

Identify the beginning, middle, and end of your story.

Recommendation #4 — Listen to someone else's story

- Find the life-changing moment.
- Listen with your ears *and* your heart.
  - o Really concentrate on what the other person is saying. Not just words, but the meaning in body language/the meaning in implied thoughts/the entire message;
  - o Remember what is being said, then build on it.
  - o Respond to the speaker in a way that will encourage.
- Be willing/open to change.
- Be open to identify something similar in your own life. Remember the stories that have made a difference in your life

and in the way you see others in the world. See the potential in others to tell those kinds of stories.

- Recognize that the stories may heal, inspire, encourage and reveal.

- Have faith and act on reconciliation.

Worksheets:
Story Starter Activities

The statements and questions found in this section are intended to stimulate your stories about race and identity and to help you find your voice. Use the worksheets as you recall details of your stories. As you remember and prepare to tell each story, ask yourself a few questions:

- Why is what happens in the story important to you?

- What do you have to lose or gain? (What's at stake in your story?)

- What did it teach you about yourself? ... or about someone else?

- What did it teach you about possibilities?

- What is the beginning, middle, end of the story? (You are developing a plot line.)

Use the prompts which follow to encourage dialogue.

Activity #1: *When I look at people I see ...*

Activity #2: *When I see police officers in my rear view mirror ...*

Activity #3:

- *I have never had a racist encounter ... OR*
- *The first racist encounter I had was ... OR*
- *The first time that I thought about race was ...*

Activity #4:

- *One time I felt small/disappointed/hurt was ...OR*
- *One time I felt strong/empowered/delighted was*

Activity #5: *I remember when I first learned that people were different…*

Activity #6: *I believe people who are ethnically different from (similar to) me …*

Activity #7: I once met a man/woman/ boy/ girl who changed me ...

Activity #8: What gives me hope is ...

Activity #9:

You may substitute any of the following and use these as story starters:

- *I remember a hate crime that I saw and turned away from …*

- *Have you ever done or witnessed something considered "racist"?*

- *Access to public space: Have you ever felt comfortable/uncomfortable (welcome/unwelcome) in a particular public space because of some part of your racial identity?*

- *Has anyone ever called you a name you don't see yourself as being? How did you feel? What did you do?*

- *Have you ever called someone else a name that is racially tinged? Recall the time.*

Understanding the Power
of Narratives to Heal

After the Storm, Then What?

Courage, my soul, and let us journey on,
Though the night is dark, it won't be very long.
Thanks be to God, the morning light appears,
And the storm is passing over, Hallelujah!

–Charles Albert Tindley

If you get enough people in the world with the right attitude,
think of how wonderful it all will be.

–Dorothy Hunt

WE DIDN'T SEE it coming. We thought we had everything covered when we left Tallahassee following a short visit in early October 2018. Not only had we cut the lawn so it looked like someone lived there, but we had reconnected with the master carpenter we met a few years before. We called him when we saw a growing crack in the carport ceiling and he came immediately – knowing we were only in town for a few days. As he pulled down the carport ceiling and started to repair what was definitely an accident-waiting- to happen, we told him we'd be leaving the next day.

"I'll handle it for you, Miss Judi," Raymond said with his heavy Southern accent, assuring us he'd complete the repairs even though we would be no where nearby.

Our house on Oak Knoll Avenue stood as it had for 60 years under the watchful eyes of four grand oak trees which predated the house.

During their long lifespan of two centuries, those oaks had seen some things. No doubt they held painful secrets no one had ever dared whisper as they stood guard on property that had once been part of a plantation that held enslaved people, was later a segregated enclave for Black professionals, and now had become one lot in a community where white and Black families lived, barely touching.

As we left on Sunday headed back to Maryland, we passed the community's newest boast awarded by the city: a sign designating Oak Knoll as Tallahassee's "Neighborhood of the Year 2018." We had only a hint that a storm would be there three days later, that it would become the third most intense hurricane ever to make landfall in the United States, that it would pack winds claiming lives and homes across its path, and that it would provide lessons in conversations.

With sustained wind speed reaching 155 miles per hour, Hurricane Michael hit Oak Knoll when we were 1300 miles away. Some neighbors had left for South Florida. Others headed north, evacuating out of Michael's path. But some stayed, braving the unprecedented Category 4 hurricane. Later they said it had been like nothing they could remember. Things went sideways. Branches snapped and fell on roofs and howling winds chilled spirits as fear drove people to huddle, wondering if it would ever end. For the rest of us – silence. Downed power lines, no electricity, no phones, no Internet which meant no contact and no news in or out. In addition, the neighborhood was physically cut off by a tree which fell across Ravine Drive – the sole access to Oak Knoll. For at least two days, those left inside couldn't get out and those outside couldn't get in. News reports showed North Florida looking like a war zone with structures down and foliage destroyed. Everybody hoped that the Weather Bureau's prediction was right, that this would be "the furious finale" to the 2018 hurricane season.

A storm may be unexpected but when it comes, it can devastate. It can uproot parts of your life and turn them into rubble. But it also has the potential to give new definitions to the concept and reality of the word "neighbor."

Reverend Larry and Dorothy Hunt are the angels who live down the street. Both are retired, he from chaplain of the Baptist Students'

Union at Florida A & M and she from teaching in public schools. Three days after the storm had passed, they called to give us an update. Every house in Oak Knoll remained standing; none had been flattened but enormous piles of debris were everywhere. One of the stately 60-foot Georgia pines in front of our house had toppled, falling directly toward the house. But miracle of miracles, it did not hit. The oak tree on the front southeast corner of the house had caught it, stopped it in its tracks, preventing the complete devastation of our home. The pine, planted by my father 60 years before, now hung precariously over the house straining to complete its trajectory yet prevented from falling by a tree whose stubbornness was legend.

"We better get this taken care of right away," Larry told us, calling from his cell phone in his house across the street that had no power. Ninety percent of Tallahassee was dark. He and Dorothy were without air, without lights, without electricity yet they thought about us. They arranged to have a commercial tree firm to remove the tree from its perch and save our house. Their faith led them to do it.

When we heard from the Hunts the next day, they had been in our yard for hours – picking up branches and supervising an impromptu clean-up before they even attempted their own. A few volunteers had come to help –white students, male and female, from nearby Florida State University, recruited by another neighbor. Who knows why they came? Perhaps the storm had pricked their consciences. (Storms have a way of doing that.) In any event, all of them worked while they talked and talked while they worked. Sometimes one on one, sometimes in small groups – Christina, Jacob, Ieva, Blake and Meg joined the Hunts. Hungry for conversation, they saw nothing off limits: family, relationships, dating experiences, the right to say no, plans for the future and even strategies to become a woman pioneer in a male dominated profession. They talked about the tartness of persimmons and the importance of getting tomato recipes before family memory disappears; they talked about job strategies and history as they filled wheelbarrow after wheelbarrow rolling nature's debris to the streets. The students were amazed at Larry's vast knowledge about each plant and its life cycle and were awed by Dorothy's creative connection with the land. And the Hunts were encouraged by the young people's willingness to help.

"Do you know what this is?" Larry asked, holding up a stalk of raw sugar cane. One of the students remembered the sweet taste from her childhood. Another had never seen or tasted it. "It's an experience," Larry laughed, urging her to try.

"Can I come back tomorrow and bring some friends?" one asked. He had been motivated and moved by both the "experience" and the genuine human compassion he felt.

Over the course of seven days, Dorothy said they learned about each other – Christina's lessons in "baking from scratch" picked up from her grandmother, the church that Larry pastored on the other side of Tallahassee, Ieva's home in Lithuania, the Black people now deceased who had once populated Oak Knoll, the students' dreams and ambitions for the future, the Hunt's commitment to service. They crossed racial and ethnic and generational and gender lines and talked about everything that meant anything to each of them. They found common ground and community in the process.

"How long have you all been married?" one student finally asked Dorothy. The inquisitive student sensed the bond of the 48-year union between the man and woman leading the clean-up. The volunteer wanted to know why the Hunts bothered to clean up someone else's yard before they cleaned their own. Their generosity screamed their philosophy as they picked up pieces of wood scattered around the yard. Raking leaves and thousands of pine cones, Dorothy showed the volunteers that marriage and being a good neighbor had something in common. They both meant working in partnership to help another.

Dorothy spoke with spiritual conviction for herself and her husband. "When you see a need, you reach out and help if you can." Then she added, "Expect nothing in return." The advice was solid. She said she knew they all wanted to stay "until the last leaf was raked."

The storm had changed the anatomy of the place. Trees looked different broken in places with fewer limbs. Piles of branches taller than humans were everywhere. Even the hedges between properties had been thinned if not completely obliterated. But after the storm, then what?

Amazingly, next to our house, tucked in its shadowed place in a space where it had surfaced before, was a single rosebud, red and ready to bloom. The storm, with all of its anger and its ugliness, with all of its fury and its force, had spared a rose.

How awesome it is that the winds can bring down a massive tree yet not touch a delicate flower. It reminds us that new connections are always possible even in the most difficult circumstances.

By the time the volunteers finished the clean-up and prepared to leave Oak Knoll, they probably sensed the power of connections and narratives – especially after this storm. Larry "gifted" them so they would remember their conversations. He took a bit of an aloe plant he had nurtured, placed pieces of it in small pots, and gave each person a plant. In traditional circles, aloe has medicinal properties. It soothes burns and heals wounds. How appropriate, then, to give aloe in a place that really needed healing. It brings hope.

Notes

- **Quote (Tutu)**: *God Has A Dream: A Vision of Hope for Our Times* by Desmond Tutu; DoubleDay, Random House, 2004.

- **Quote (Evans)**: *I am a Black Woman (Poems by Mari Evans);* Writers and Readers Publishing, 1971.

Part I - On Petals, Stems and Thorns...

- **Quote (Barber)**: "When Silence is Not an Option" (sermon)– Rev. Dr. William J Barber II; Riverside Church, New York City; 2016. https://www.facebook.com/RevDrBarber/videos/when-silence-is-not-an-option-rev-dr-william-j-barber-ii-speaks-at-the-historic-/1255270804592790/

- **Quote (Black)**: *The Coming: A Novel* by Daniel Black; St. Martin's Press, New York, 2015.

ROSE POEM

- **Quote (Bethune)**: Mary McLeod Bethune https://www.azquotes.com/author/1352-Mary_McLeod_Bethune

CHAPTER: *THE ROSE*

- **Quote (Tutu)**: *God Has A Dream: A Vision of Hope for Our Times* by Desmond Tutu; DoubleDay, Random House, 2004.

CHAPTER: *MOVIE THEATRE TRUTH*

- **Quote (Marshall)**: "The Liberty Medal Acceptance Speech" delivered by Thurgood Marshall; Philadelphia, PA; July 4, 1992.

CHAPTER: *FIRST JOB*

- **Quote (King)**: "The Other America" (speech) delivered by Martin Luther King, jr. Grosse Pointe High School, March 1968.

CHAPTER: *LOOK ALIKE*

- **Quote (West)**: Speech delivered By Dr. Cornel West at Riverside RCC, 2010.

- **She had come . . . .** : The college once known as Hampton Institute is now Hampton University in Virginia.

- **We heard music differently** . . . . : Studies of ethnic groups suggest that audiences respond differently to a 4/4 rhythm based upon cultural experiences. African Americans tend to clap on 2 and 4 (back beat or down beat) while white audiences tend to clap on 1 and 3. Syncopation emerged as an African American rhythmic device known as the back beat (in traditional African American musical genres: jazz, gospel, blues, ragtime.) http://www.louisianafolklife.org/LT/Articles_Essays/clap_on_2_4.html (Kalamu ya Salaam, "Clapping on Two and Four").

CHAPTER: *A HAIR STORY*

- **Quote (Hurston)**: *Dust Tracks on a Road: An Autobiography* by Zora Neale Hurston; J.B. Lippincott, USA, 1942.

CHAPTER: *NUDE STOCKINGS*

- **Quote (Fish):** *The Myth of Race* by Jefferson M. Fish, Ph.D., published by Argo Navis, November 2012.

CHAPTER: *THE OBLIGATION TO SPEAK*

- **Quote (Douglass):** Frederick Douglass, in a statement on behalf of delegates to the National Colored Convention held in Rochester, New York, in July 1853.

- **Quote (Weatherford):** Jeffery Weatherford, Howard University, in conversation backstage at "Howard's Hottest" (a production of WHBC), 2016.

Part II – Story Hope

- **Quote (Alexander):** Michelle Alexander - in conversation – Haymarket Books, Chicago, May 9, 2017. https://truthout.org/articles/people-were-resisting-before-trump-michelle-alexander-naomi-klein-and-keeanga-yamahtta-taylor-in-conversation/

CHAPTER: *THE RHODA (ROSE) SPIRIT*

- **Quote (West):** Excerpted from the Ware lecture delivered by Cornel West at Unitarian Universalist Association 2015.

- **In the Christian Bible, the story of Peter** . . . : This story is found in Acts 12 of the Bible. Peter, a follower of Jesus Christ and leader of the church in Jerusalem, had been imprisoned for speaking and preaching the new religion. Held in chains and under the watchful eye of dozens of jailers, he had been sentenced to death. But on the night before his scheduled execution, an angel of the Lord arrived, led him out of the maximum-security facility, and directed him to the home of Mary where church members were praying.

CHAPTER: *ROSES IN THE WILDERNESS*

- **Quote (Barber):** "Rev. Barber on Hope"; Statement by Rev. Dr. William J. Barber on YouTube; Poor People's Campaign: A National Call for Moral Revival; May 23, 2017. https://www.youtube.com/watch?v=kLxgd5ACaK8

- **It's not clear whether he told them the mantra . . . :** This is a cultural expression passed from one generation to another among African Americans. It describes a condition reflecting a bias against African Americans that assumes they will be discriminated against no matter what they do.

- **One day they would be professionals . . . :** From a speech by John W. Davis delivered on the campus of West Virginia State College, 1932. This speech is housed in the John W. Davis Papers, Moorland-Spingarn Collection, Howard University, Washington, D.C.

- **And then in Georgia, a prominent woman . . . :** Juliette Dericotte, Dean of Women at Fisk University in Tennessee, was an African American educator and activist. As she rode in a car with three students in Atlanta, a white driver forced her off the road into a ditch. Her injuries from the accident were severe and racist policies in the South denied her access to hospital care. She died hours after the tragedy.

- **They may have resented his co-founding Meharry . . . :** Meharry Medical College was founded in 1876 as the medical department at Central Tennessee College. It later became the first medical school in the South for African Americans.

- **Despite potential calamity . . . :** From a speech by John W. Davis delivered on the campus of West Virginia State College, 1932. (This speech is housed in the Moorland-Spingarn Collection, Howard University.)

- **As you think, think of the wilderness . . . :** Isaiah 35:1 - "The wilderness and the solitary place shall be glad for them; and the desert shall rejoice, and blossom as the rose." This scripture verse was referenced by Dr. John W. Davis in a speech delivered in 1932. Davis said, "The statement is supposed to represent ... succeeding under difficult circumstances." (Moorland-Spingarn Collection, Howard University.)

CHAPTER: *A COLLECTIVE WILL*

- **Quote (Angelou):** Angelou's FaceBook page, January 11, 2013.

CHAPTER: *THE EYES HAVE IT – MAHALA AND SAM*

- **Quote (Moore):** Letter from Oscar Moore in Tallahassee, Florida to Judi Moore and Jacqui Malone in Hampton, Virginia, 1966.

- **A perpetual "yes" embedded in their eyes blended their "mustard seed" faith** . . . : In the Christian tradition, faith is a strong belief in the tremendous power of God. Two stories (in Matthew 17:20 and Luke 17:5-6) of the New Testament of the Bible describe a believer who only needs a miniscule amount of faith—"the size of a mustard seed" to "move mountains" and to do other things believed impossible. "Mustard seed faith" references a belief that the Biblical teachings live.

CHAPTER: *THREE MEDITATIONS ON BEING SIX*

- **Quote (Rumi):** Julaluddin Rumi was a 13th century Persian poet, theologian and scholar whose works were translated widely. https://quotecites.com/quote/Rumi_7848

- **Yet, in 2013, only 256 of the 3,200 children's books** . . . : Excerpted from the Study by the Cooperative Children's Book Center, University of Wisconsin. 2013; http://ccbc.education. wisc.edu/books/pcstats.asp

- **By 2016, the numbers . . .:**

http://www.npr.org/sections/
codeswitch/2017/02/17/515792141/authors-and-illustrators-of-col-
or-accounted-for-22-percent-of-children-s-books

CHAPTER: *CALVIN BESS' FOOTSTEPS*

- **Quote (Due)**: Words memorialized on Sidewalk Footsteps tribute to "Foot Soldiers of the Movement"; corner of Jefferson Street and Adams Street; Tallahassee, Florida; observed 2016.

- **In fact, a later account of his life** . . . : Tananarive Due and Patricia Stephens Due, *Freedom in the Family: A Mother-Daughter Memoir of the Fight for Civil Rights*. Random House, 2009.

- **The family took it the hardest** . . . : In the summer of 2016, I had conversations with others who knew Calvin Bess. Among those interviewed were: Dr. Mabel Sherman, FAMU High choir director and music teacher who sang "The Lord's Prayer" at Calvin's funeral and Rev. Dr. Henry Marion Steele who graduated from FAMU High in 1961 one year before Calvin.

- **They had become a part of the national conversation** . . . : Due, *Freedom in the Family: A Mother-Daughter Memoir of the Fight for Civil Rights*.

CHAPTER: *WHEN MOM TALKED WITH HER TOES*

- **Quote (Groopman)**: *The Anatomy of Hope: How People Prevail in the Face of Illness* by Jerome Groopman, MD; Random House Publishing; Random House, Inc., New York; 2004.

CHAPTER: AND THERE WAS ONE

- **Quote (Black)**: *The Coming: A Novel* by Daniel Black; St. Martin's Press, New York, 2015.

CHAPTER: *IF IT HAPPENED ONCE ON ROBBEN ISLAND*

- **Quote (Angelou):** "On the Pulse of Morning" – poem delivered by Maya Angelou at the Inauguration of Bill Clinton as the 42nd President of the United States; Washington, DC; January 20, 1993.

- **"Here you will die"** . . . : Nelson Mandela, *Long Walk to Freedom: The Autobiography of Nelson Mandela*, Little Brown & Co., 1994.

- **He may have told me** . . . : On three successive trips to South Africa between 2000 and 2011, I met and talked with white South Africans who worked in government, education and private industry in Capetown, Johannesburg, Durban and Bloemfontein.

- **In the days following apartheid** . . . : Nelson Mandela, *Long Walk to Freedom: The Autobiography of Nelson Mandela*, Little Brown & Co., 1994.

Part III - Toward a Conversation

- **Quote (Cooper):** From the current U.S. Passport - Note–Anna J. Cooper is the only woman and the only African American quoted on the U.S. Passport.

- **Quote (Barber):** Rev. Dr. William J. Barber at Howard University, Fall 2017.

CHAPTER: *A TOOL KIT: A STORY-HOPE PRIMER*

- **Quote (Tutu):** *No Future Without Forgiveness* by Desmond Tutu; Random House, Inc.; New York, New York; 1999.

- **Ubuntu: I am because of you** . . . : "Ubuntu" is an Nguni Bantu phrase popularized by South African humanists. It appeared in both written and spoken texts by South African leaders including *No Future without Forgiveness*, Desmond Tutu, 1999.

- **As the writer** . . . : Chimamanda Ngozi Adichie, *Dear Ijewele, or A Feminist Manifesto in Fifteen Suggestions*, Alfred A. Knopf, 2017.

- **Research shows that if we can find** . . . : Dr. Drew Westen, Emory University, *Four Freedoms Fund (How to Talk to Americans about Demographic Change and Unconscious Bias)*.

CHAPTER: *AFTER THE STORM, THEN WHAT?*

- **Quote (Tindley)**: "The Storm is Passing Over" (hymn lyrics) – composed by Charles Albert Tindley, 1851.

Acknowledgements

I NEVER WOULD HAVE known about the rose had not Dorothy Hunt sent me a photo. I'm grateful for the repeated photos she sent for 4 straight years and for the friendship with Larry and Dorothy that surrounded and preceded the pictures. I am grateful too for the writers of the Bethesda Writers Group who read and massaged these stories: Bonnie Miller, Ken Ackerman, Michael Scadron, Michael Kirkland, Diana Parsell, Sonja Williams and especially Cheryl LaRoche who nudged me and Nancy Durr who insisted that the Tool Kit be tried.

To Raven Padgett, my extraordinary editor who read with care and to Dackeyia Sterling who knows how to pull stories and make books happen … thank you.

To my academic community at Howard University—colleagues and students who embraced the work without even realizing it … thank you.

To all of those who prayed mightily that I might teach others how to tell stories, including my friends at the Olive Branch Community Church, the saints on the Hemingway Temple morning prayer line, the women of Women and the Word, and the countless others who know the words of prayer and spoke them… thank you.

To those among my other friends: Freeman and Jackie Hrabowski who sent regular encouragement; Dianne Boardley Suber who insisted on claiming Tallahassee; The Flowers clan who welcomed me home to Florida as I wrote; Mel, Jacqui (Sug), Linda, Tootie and Darryl whose conversations sent me in search of identity… thank you.

To all who read/heard/tried bits of this work and gave feedback including Lebo M. from South Africa; the late Catherine Gira, former chair of the Maryland Humanities Council; Pam Ferrell, Laverne Wilson; Paul Coates, Vicci Saunders... thank you.

To family who inspired and gave me hope: my children Nikole, Lauren and John; my grandchildren John II, Jazmine, Makenzie and Sydney; and my beloved parents who rest in heaven ... thank you.

To the love of my life who wouldn't let go until this idea flowered, who read every word and prayed me to completion, my husband and partner Joe ... thank you.

You are all a blessing!

About the Author

Judi Moore Latta, Ph.D., is a storyteller who calls herself one of the "GRITS" (Girls Raised in the South). A native of Tallahassee, Florida, she is an award-winning journalist and retired professor of communications. For more than three decades she worked at Howard University in Washington, DC, serving on the faculty and in the administration in various capacities including as Executive Director of Communications and Marketing for the University for three years. As a veteran media professional, she has worked in public and commercial broadcasting as a manager, writer and producer. She served as National Public Radio's first education reporter and earned the George Foster Peabody Award as senior producer of the 26-part documentary series, *Wade in the Water: African American Sacred Music Traditions*. For dozens of productions, she has received recognition from the Corporation for Public Broadcasting, American Women in Radio and Television, National Education Association, National Association of Black Journalists and National Federation of Community Broadcasters.

She graduated from Hampton Institute, earned a Masters in English from Boston University and a Ph.D. from the University of Maryland College Park. She lives with her husband Joseph Latta, D.D.S. in Silver Spring, Maryland.

Other work by Judi Moore Latta

God Ain't Sleep: Yesterday, Today and Tomorrow

Made in the USA
Columbia, SC
19 February 2020

88150088R00074